GETTING TO KNOW THE UNITED STATES

☆☆☆☆☆☆☆☆☆☆☆☆☆☆☆☆☆☆☆☆☆☆☆☆☆☆☆☆☆☆☆☆☆

The History of the United States

Volume 1

☆☆☆☆☆☆☆☆☆☆☆☆☆☆☆☆☆☆☆☆☆☆☆☆☆☆☆☆☆☆☆☆☆

Robert J. Field

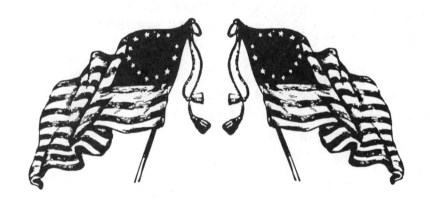

BOOK-LAB
P.O. Box 230206, New York, NY 10023-0206

© 1998 Robert J. Field
    Skokie, Illinois

BOOK LAB
PO Box 230206
New York, NY 10023-0206
Telephones 212 874-5534 . 800 654-4081
Telefax 212 874-3105
EMail BOOKLABpub@AOL.com

The History of the United States, Vol. 1 Textbook hardcover
7570 ISBN 87594-370-5

The History of the United States, Vol. 2 Textbook hardcover
7571 ISBN 87594-371-3

The History of the United States, Teacher's Guide
7575 ISBN 87594-372-1

The History of the United States, Volume 1 workbook
7576 ISBN 87594-379-9

The History of the United States, Volume 2 workbook
7577 ISBN 87594-374-8

Text design & production: Tobi R. Krutt
Cover design & text maps: Lloyd Birmingham

Photo acknowledgements: 2: Library of Congress; 8: Library of Congress;
19: New York Public Library; 34: Library of Congress; 47: Library of
Congress; 53: Library of Congress; 56: New York Public Library; 85: Library
of Congress; 101: Library of Congress

Printed in the United States of America

Table of Contents

1

Explorers

KEY WORDS

continent   A large land area. A *continent* does not have one government. Europe and Asia are *continents.*

country   A part of a continent with a government. Our *country* is the United States of America.

government   A group of officials that rules a country, state, or city. Our country's *government* protects us.

explorer   A person who travels in places that are unknown. An *explorer* wants to know more about these unknown places. Christopher Columbus was an *explorer.*

Indies   The Far East; the part of Asia where India and China are. Many people from Europe wanted spices from the *Indies.*

king   A man who rules a country. Most *kings* have all the power in a country. Their job is handed down to their children. *King* Ferdinand ruled Spain.

queen   A woman who rules a country or is the wife of a king. *Queen* Isabella ruled Spain with King Ferdinand.

New World   North and South America. The part of the world that people from Europe did not know until Columbus discovered the *New World.*

sail   To make a trip on a ship. Columbus *sailed* west to go to India.

compass   A thing that shows where you are going. Columbus used a *compass* to sail west.

Columbus landing in the New World

2

FINDING A NEW WORLD

For years, people heard stories about the Far East. Marco Polo went to Asia by going east over the mountains. He went to China. It was a long trip and took many years. When he came back to Italy he brought silk and spices. He also told stories about the riches of India and China.

People in Europe wanted the riches of the Far East. These riches were in China and India, two countries in the eastern part of Asia. Exciting things were in China and India, so people in Europe wanted to go there. They wanted to get silk and spices from the East. But the East was very far and hard to get to. There were huge mountains and deserts to cross.

Christopher Columbus lived in Europe in the 1400s. He was born in the city of Genoa, which is a seaport in Italy. Columbus had been a sailor for a long time. He had a new idea about how to get to east Asia. He would sail west. Most people thought that Columbus was crazy. "Ships sail close to shore," they said. Columbus answered: "With my trusty compass I can cross the ocean."

To get to India, Columbus sailed west on the Atlantic Ocean. No one had sailed so far west before. His crew was afraid. Some of the crew wanted to turn back, but Columbus kept going. He believed in his idea. He was sure they would soon find India.

When he landed, Columbus was surprised by the people. They did not look like people from Asia. But he called them "Indians" because he thought he landed in the Indies.

Columbus found a "new world." That is why we call North America, Central America, and South America the *New World*. But Columbus did not know this. He was sure that he landed in the Indies.

FILL IN THE RIGHT ANSWER

Find these answers in the story.

1. Columbus sailed _____ to get to India. *(east, west)*
2. He sailed on the _____ Ocean. *(Atlantic, Pacific)*
3. His crew was _____. *(cheerful, afraid)*
4. Columbus was _____ that he was right. *(sad, sure)*
5. The crew was glad to see _____. *(night, land)*
6. Columbus was surprised when he landed. The people did not look like _____. *(people from Asia, Russians)*
7. Columbus thought that he landed in the _____. *(Indies, Pacific Ocean)*
8. Columbus really found a new _____. *(world, earth)*
9. Columbus called the people _____ because he thought that he landed in India. *(French, Indians)*
10. The people did not understand Columbus because they spoke a different _____. *(language, tune)*

FACT OR OPINION

A *fact* is something that is true.
An *opinion* is how a person feels about something.

Example: There are seven days in one week. (FACT)
Sunday is the best day in the week. (OPINION)

Here are some sentences. They are either facts or opinions.

Write "F" for facts. Write "O" for opinions.

1. The United States has fifty states._____
2. There are twelve months in a year._____
3. Florida is the best state in the United States._____
4. President Kennedy was our best president._____
5. Columbus' ideas were crazy._____
6. Columbus was not old enough to sail to the New World._____
7. Marco Polo was smarter than Columbus._____
8. Columbus' ships had sails._____
9. China and India are in Asia._____
10. Columbus found something more important than spices and silk._____

4

NEWSPAPERS

WHICH WORD FITS?

Choose the right word.

Today we read news from newspapers. There were no newspapers in the 1400s. This is the time of Columbus. The printing press was just invented. Few people went to school. So most people could not _____.

a. race	c. read
b. red	d. run

The first newspapers were hard to read. They had small print. They did not have pictures. Today, newspapers have photographs. Headlines are the main idea in a newspaper story. Headlines have very large print. The story under the headlines has smaller _____.

a. place	c. pints
b. print	d. points

There are many newspapers today. Most cities have at least one newspaper. Bigger cities have two or three. Many people read _____ every day. Newspapers give more news than TV. But they have many things besides news. People also read them for fun.

a. nuts	c. naps
b. newspapers	d. needs

What Newspapers Have

Stores that want to sell things buy advertisements. A shorter word for advertisements is "ads." Stores pay a lot of money for these ads. There are two main kinds of ads in newspapers. Big ads fill a whole page or a big part of the page. Classified ads are small. They are only a few lines long. They are much cheaper. People use want ads to tell what they want to buy or sell. The ads help to pay for the newspaper.

A good newspaper gives *facts* in its news sections. It tells its *opinions* in the "editorial" section.

Here are just a few of the things that modern newspapers have:

News	Movie news	Advertisements
Sports	Puzzles	Business news
TV lists	Big Ads	Classified ads (want ads)
Ann Landers	Dear Abby	Horoscopes
Weather	Travel	Book section
Horoscopes	Hobbies	Editorials

FILL IN THE RIGHT ANSWER

1. Newspapers give_____ (facts, trouble, money) and _____ (food, opinion,. direction.)

2. Facts are in the _____ (editorial, news, ads) section.

3. Opinions are in the _____ (editorial, news, ads) section.

4. Stores tell about their products in the _____ (editorial, news, ads) part of the paper.

5. Big stores often run _____ (classified, full page, sports) ads to sell their products.

6. _____ (Classified, short, big-time) ads are cheaper.

7. Baseball and football scores are found in the _____ (classified, news, sports) section.

8. Sometimes we want to know if it will rain. That information is in the _____ (editorial, news, weather) section of the paper.

9. Many people look in the newspaper to see what time _____ (animals, drums, movies) are playing.

Newspapers Tell About Columbus

We know that there were no real newspapers when Columbus planned his trips. Let us pretend that we have two newspapers from that time. The newspapers have different *opinions* on Columbus' ideas.

Here is how they might look.

Spanish News

August 6, 1492

Price **5 Centavos**

A Foolish Idea

Christopher Columbus is a man from Genoa. He thinks that the world is round. Columbus really believes that he can reach India by going west. Everybody knows that the world is flat.

Now Columbus tries to get money from Queen Isabella to try out his silly idea.

What a waste of money! Spain has better things to do with its money.

Who wants to go on such a dangerous trip? Only crazy people want to fall off the edge of the world.

Why doesn't Columbus get his money from Genoa if his ideas are so good?

A New Idea

We all know about the treasures of China and India. But India and China are east of Spain. It is a long, hard trip from Spain to China. You have to cross huge mountains and it is dangerous.

Now a brave explorer has a new idea. He thinks that he has a shortcut to China and India. Christopher Columbus believes that with the help of his compass he can go west across the ocean and find India. No one has done that before.

Spain is lucky that Columbus came here for the money. This will give Spain a chance to be the richest country in Europe. Columbus is very brave. We wish him good luck.

The newspapers have different opinions on Columbus' ideas.

Columbus presenting plans to Queen Isabella

FILL IN THE RIGHT ANSWER

Write "News" after each statement that agrees with the *Spanish News*.
Write "Press" after each statement that agrees with the *Spanish Press*.

1. Columbus should go back to Genoa and leave Spain alone.
_____

2. Columbus does not know what he is talking about. _____
3. Spain is lucky to have Columbus. _____
4. Queen Isabella should give Columbus money. _____
5. People are crazy if they go with Columbus on his trip. _____

REMEMBER — Today's newspapers give their *opinions* on the editorial page. The news pages are supposed to have only *facts*.

SOMETHING TO THINK ABOUT

We say that Columbus *discovered* America. He did not really discover it. People were already living in the "New World." Today we call these people "native Americans" because they were really the first Americans. Columbus only "discovered" America for the European countries.

The land belonged to the people he called "Indians." Indians were not all the same. They belonged to different tribes. Each tribe was like a separate country and had its own language and ways of life.

Leif Ericson was a Viking. Many people say that he was the first European to find the "New World." But he did not do much about it. When Columbus found America it "stayed discovered." Europeans paid attention to Columbus' discovery. They explored the land. Some Europeans came to the New World to stay.

1. Why are the "Indians" Columbus found really "native Americans?"
2. Why was Columbus' discovery more important than Leif Ericson's?
3. Were all American Indians alike? Explain.

WRITE A LETTER

Pretend that Columbus forgot to finish this letter to Queen Isabella. Finish the letter. Fill in the blanks with the right word.

The Indies
October 12, 1492

Queen Isabella
Queen's Castle
Madrid, Spain

Dear Queen Isabella:

I bring you great news! We _____ (logged, landed) in the Indies today. We are happy to see land again. The _____ (crew, crow) was scared all week. Many of them still thought the earth was _____ (full, flat). They were afraid that we would _____ (fool, fall) off the edge of the world.

The people here are _____ (fakers, friendly). We did not find any _____ (rifles, riches) yet. These natives do not look like the people that _____ (Marco Polo, Mr. Moto) saw in Asia. It is hard to talk to them. They have their own _____ (leather, language). They do not speak _____ (Swedish, Spanish).

I hope that you are _____ (pleased, poor) with our discovery. We proved that people can go west from Spain and get to the _____. (Inches, Indies.) This also proves that we can _____ (sail, smile) across the ocean.

We know that our discovery will bring glory to _____ (Stain, Spain).

Your servant,
Christopher Columbus

CONTINENTS, COUNTRIES, AND CITIES

Europe is a *continent*. A continent is a large land area. A *country* is part of a continent. Europe has many countries. Some countries in Europe are: England, France, Spain, Italy, and Germany.

A *government* is a group of people who run a country. Each country has its own government. Continents do not have governments.

Countries have cities. A *city* is a place where a lot of people live and work. New York City is a large city in the United States. In England, London is a big city. The large city of Paris is in France. Barcelona, which is a large city, is in Spain. Rome is a big city in Italy and the large city of Berlin is in Germany.

North America is the continent on which we live. The United States is in North America and is our country. Our country has a government. The government's main offices are in the city of Washington, D. C.. This city is the capital of our country.

FILL IN THE RIGHT ANSWER

1. A c_____t is a large land area.
2. Continents have c_____s in them.
3. Our continent is N_____h A_____a.
4. The name of our country is the U_____d S_____s.
5. Countries have c_____s.
6. Every country has a c_____l.
7. The capital of the United States is W_____n, _____.
8. The g_____t of a country is in the capital.
9. Governments r_____n their countries.
10. A place where a lot of people live and work is a c_____y.

DIRECTIONS ON MAPS

The directions on a map are North, South, East, and West. The earth is round but a map is flat. You have to fold a map to see that the Pacific ocean continues from one end of the map to the other. You can see the difference between a flat map and a round one on a globe.

Write the correct direction. Look at the map and the part of the map that tells directions.

1. North America is _____ of South America.
2. Asia is _____ of Europe.
3. On this map, North America is _____ of Europe.
4. Europe is _____ of North America.
5. Africa is _____ of Europe.

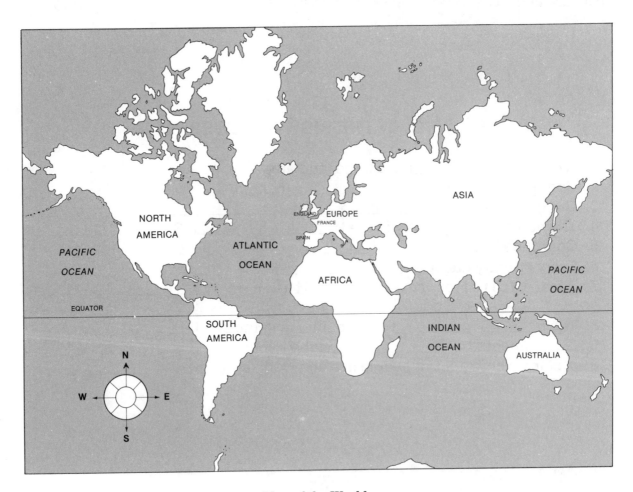

Map of the World

LEARNING THE LANGUAGE

NOUNS

Nouns are names of persons, places, or things.

Underline the nouns in each sentence. A sentence might have more than one noun.

Example: We ate the cake.
Henry Smith drove his car to his house.

1. Columbus was wise.
2. Three ships sailed.
3. The Indians were friendly to the sailors.
4. Many countries wanted to explore the New World.
5. Queen Isabella gave Columbus money.
6. The trip lasted a long time.
7. Many people thought that Columbus was wrong.
8. Portugal took the land that is now Brazil.
9. Newspapers tell us what is happening in the world.
10. They did not find gold.

SOME LATER EXPLORERS

After Columbus discovered the New World other people sailed across the oceans. They too were explorers.

Balboa

Vasco Balboa was born in Spain and was very poor. He always wanted to be a sailor because he loved adventure. One day, Balboa hid on a ship bound for the New World. The captain of the ship was looking for gold in South America. He caught Balboa hiding on the ship and was very angry.

The ship landed in what is now Colombia. Balboa fought with the captain, won, and took over the crew. Now Balboa was captain.

When Balboa asked the Indians for gold, they could not understand him. Finally, Balboa showed the Indians a piece of gold. Now they understood. The Indians told Balboa to go west and look for a great sea.

Balboa had to go through the jungle for sixty miles. It was hot and he did not find gold. But, when he climbed a hill, he saw something that made his heart beat faster.

Balboa saw the giant Pacific Ocean. He was the first European to see it.

FILL IN THE RIGHT ANSWER

Find these answers in the story.

1. Balboa loved the _____. *(see, sea)*
2. Balboa _____ on the ship. *(hid, hide)*
3. The captain was _____ with Balboa. *(afraid, angry)*
4. Balboa was the first European to see the _____ Ocean. *(Atlantic, Pacific)*
5. Balboa was looking for _____. *(good, gold)*

Magellan Sails Around the World

Ferdinand Magellan led the first trip around the world. He was from Portugal. But he sailed for the king of Spain. Portugal is Spain's neighbor. Portugal is west of Spain.

Magellan read about Balboa's discovery of the Pacific Ocean. This gave him an idea. He wanted to sail all the way around the world. This was a brave idea.

Magellan sailed across the Atlantic and Pacific Oceans. The trip was very long. Many men died. There was not enough food. Finally he landed in what is now the Philippine Islands.

Magellan died in the Philippine Islands. One of his ships reached Spain in 1522. It went around the world. The trip took three years. It is too bad that Magellan did not live to see it.

WHICH WORD FITS?

1. Many men _____ on Magellan's voyage. *(died, danced)*
2. The men were hungry because there was not enough _____. *(fists, food)*
3. Magellan landed in what is now the _____ Islands. *(Pacific, Philippine)*
4. Magellan _____ in the Philippine Islands. *(died, danced)*
5. One of Magellan's _____ sailed around the world. *(ships, shapes)*
6. Magellan did not _____ to see his idea become true. *(lie, live)*
7. It took the ship about three years to sail around the _____. *(wheel, world)*

15

John Cabot

John Cabot explored for England. But he was born in Genoa, the city in which Columbus was born. John Cabot sold spices. Like Columbus, he wanted to find a shortcut to the Indies. But he wanted to go Northwest. He thought that way was faster than Columbus' trip.

Cabot went to England for money. He told some English spice sellers that he would make them rich. They gave him money for his trip. It was easier now to get money to go across the Atlantic Ocean. Columbus showed that it was safe.

King Henry VII agreed to let Cabot sail for England. Cabot sailed on May 2, 1497. He took only one ship with eighteen men aboard. The ship landed on June 24, 1497. Cabot claimed the land as "New found land." The name stuck. It is still called "Newfoundland." Today, it is part of Canada.

Explorers kept records of their trips. These records are called "logs." Cabot did not keep good records. He wrote very little in his logs. This made it hard for people to believe him.

Cabot went to Newfoundland again a year later. This time he took five ships. He also took his son, Sebastian, with him. John Cabot did not come back. Sebastian tried to take credit for his father's discoveries. Sebastian also kept poor records. Experts found that the credit belonged to John Cabot.

FILL IN THE RIGHT ANSWER

Find these answers in the story.

1. John Cabot was born in _____. *(Genoa, Germany)*
2. He sold _____. *(specials, spices)*
3. Cabot wanted to find a shortcut to the _____. *(Inches, Indies)*
4. He wanted to go _____ to get to the Indies. *(Northwest, Nowhere)*
5. Cabot went to _____ sellers for money. *(sports, spice)*
6. Cabot did not keep good _____ of his trip. *(reeds, records)*
7. Cabot called his discovery _____. *(Newfoundland, New York)*
8. Today Cabot's discovery is part of _____. *(California, Canada)*
9. Cabot took his son on a second _____. *(trip, trap)*
10. Sebastian tried to take _____ for John Cabot's discoveries. *(credit, crew)*

Jacques Cartier

Jacques Cartier was born in France. Like Cabot, he wanted to find a northern route to Asia. This northern route is called the "Northwest Passage." Cartier sailed for the king of France.

Cartier left France on April 20, 1534. He took sixty-one men on two small ships.

Cartier landed in Newfoundland. But he went farther than Cabot. Cartier wanted to sail across the North American continent by going west. He crossed the Gulf of St. Lawrence. But he came to a dead end. The river was blocked.

Cartier made friends with two Indians. These Indians called their home "Canada." The Indians told Cartier to go farther west.

Jacques Cartier claimed the land for France. But he was sad. He found out that the St. Lawrence River did not go to Asia.

Cartier went back to France. But the king of France still thought that the St. Lawrence River led to Asia. So he sent Cartier back to Canada. Cartier went farther west this time. But he was unhappy. He still did not find Asia.

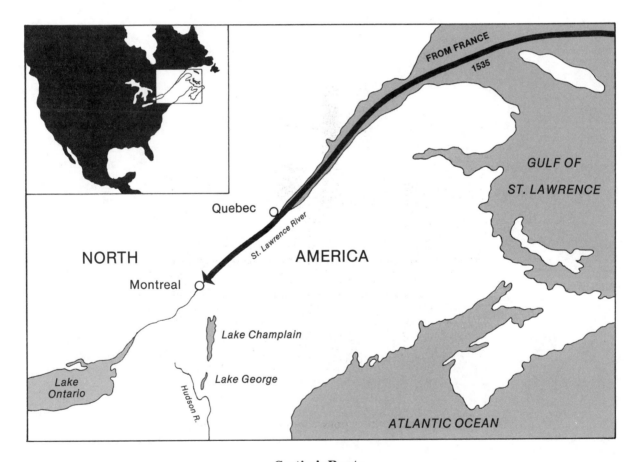

Cartier's Route

TRUE OR FALSE

Read the story again.
Write *T* if the statement is true.
Write *F* if the statement is false.

Example: Jacques Cartier was English. _____F_____

1. Jacques Cartier was born in Spain. _____
2. Cartier sailed for the king of France. _____
3. Cartier wanted to sail southwest. _____
4. Cartier landed in Newfoundland. _____
5. Cabot went farther than Cartier. _____
6. The king of France sent Cartier back to Canada. _____
7. The Indians did not like Cartier. _____
8. Cartier reached Asia on his first trip. _____
9. Cartier reached Asia on his second trip. _____
10. Cartier wanted to go west on the Mississippi River. _____

Cartier taking possession of New France

Marquette and Joliet

France was still looking for a river that led to Asia. French leaders heard of a huge river – the Mississippi River. France wanted Father Marquette and Louis Joliet to see if this river led to Asia.

Father Marquette was a young French priest. He was one of France's best explorers. He lived with the Indians. He tried to teach them the Christian religion. Father Marquette learned the Indians' language and customs. Louis Joliet was a fur trader. They explored together. They went all the way to the Mississippi River. Then they sailed down the Mississippi.

Marquette and Joliet started on their search in 1673. Marquette's friendship with the Indians helped him. Indian guides went with Marquette and Joliet. The Indians were expert guides. They knew the land very well. It was their home land.

Marquette and Joliet sailed down the Mississippi River. They saw many wonderful things. There were many furry animals. The land was beautiful.

But they were unhappy. They saw that they were sailing south and they knew that Asia was west. But they continued their trip until they reached another river. This was the Missouri River. This river did go west. But they decided to continue sailing on the Mississippi River.

Marquette and Joliet decided that the Mississippi River flowed into the Gulf of Mexico. They were right. Look at the map.

Marquette and Joliet helped France. Now France claimed much land in the New World.

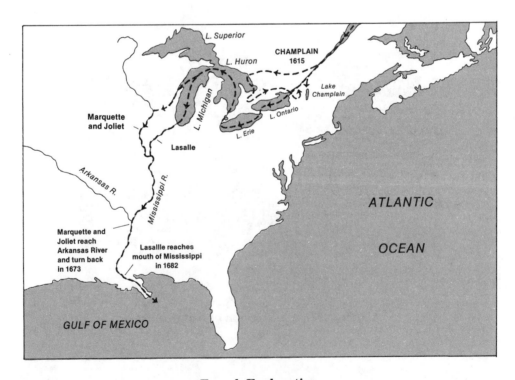

French Exploration

WHICH WORD FITS?

Read these words. They are from the story. Pick the word that fits the sentence.

fur trader	guides	Mississippi	Missouri
Asia	priest	friendly	land
west	France	south	courage

1. Father Marquette was a _____.
2. Louis Joliet was a _____.
3. Father Marquette was _____ with the Indians.
4. Marquette and Joliet sailed down the _____ River.
5. France was looking for a river that led to _____.
6. Indian _____ went with Marquette and Joliet.
7. Marquette and Joliet saw that they were sailing _____ on the Mississippi River.
8. They knew that they had to go _____ to get to Asia.
9. Marquette and Joliet reached another river while they sailed on the Mississippi. This was the _____ River.
10. Marquette and Joliet helped France claim much _____ in the New World.

Henry Hudson

Henry Hudson was an Englishman. But he explored in North America for Holland. Hudson headed for the New World in 1609. His ship was called the "Half Moon." He too wanted to find a river that crossed North America to Asia.

Hudson sailed to what is now New York. He sailed up a river. This river is now called the "Hudson River." Hudson hoped this river led across North America. But he could not go very far. He came to dangerous rapids. These rapids were very strong. They were near what is now Albany, New York.

Hudson explored this area. He claimed a large part of land—the Hudson River valley. People from Holland settled in this area. An important city in Holland is Amsterdam. They called their city "New Amsterdam." Later, the name was changed to New York.

TRUE OR FALSE

Read the story of Henry Hudson again.
Write *T* if the statement is true.
Write *F* if the statement is false.

Example: People who live in Holland are called
Dutch people. _____T_____

1. Amsterdam is a city in England. _____
2. Henry Hudson wanted to find a river that crossed North America. _____
3. Henry Hudson was Dutch. _____
4. Today New Amsterdam is called New York. _____
5. People from Holland settled in the Hudson River valley. _____

22

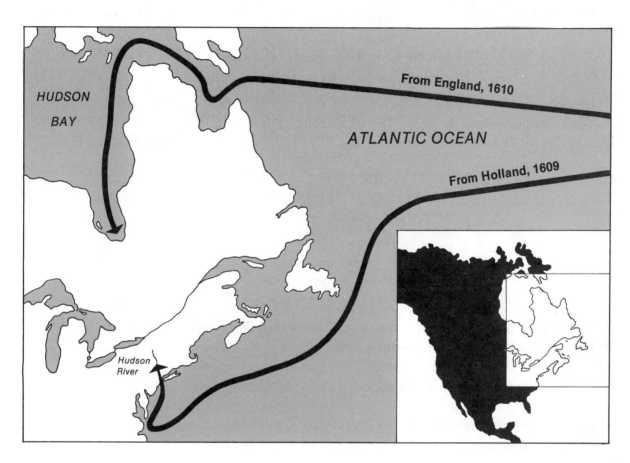

Hudson's Exploration

WHICH WORD FITS?

Fill in the right explorers:

Columbus	Balboa	Marquette and Joliet
Cartier	Magellan	Cabot
	Hudson	

1. _____ led the first trip around the world.
2. _____ called his discovery "Newfoundland."
3. _____ discovered the Pacific Ocean.
4. _____ discovered land that became New Amsterdam.
5. _____ found that the Mississippi River went to the Gulf of Mexico.
6. _____ was the first to discover the New World for Spain.
7. _____ sailed in the "Half Moon" to find a river that went across North America.

Fill in the correct country for each explorer. Tell which country sent the explorer — NOT where he was born.

Spain	France	England	Holland

1. Christopher Columbus _____
2. Henry Hudson _____
3. John Cabot _____
4. Ferdinand Magellan _____
5. Father Marquette _____
6. Louis Joliet _____
7. Jacques Cartier _____
8. Vasco Balboa _____

LEARNING THE LANGUAGE
Plurals

We usually add the letter "s" to a word to show more than one. We call this the "plural" of the word.

Example: I have a *map*. (one map)
We have ten *maps*. (more than one)

Add the letter "s" to each word to make it more than one.
Example: I like to eat *eggs*. (egg)

1. Balboa loved _____. *(ship)*
2. Columbus made four _____ to the New World. *(trip)*
3. Balboa asked the _____ for directions. *(Indian)*
4. People in Europe only knew of three _____ before the New World was discovered. *(continent)*
5. Some people did not believe Columbus' new _____. *(idea)*
6. The Atlantic and Pacific are two large _____. *(ocean)*
7. _____ are also called trips. *(Voyage)*
8. Columbus had to have good _____ to complete his trips. *(instrument)*
9. Columbus knew how to make _____. *(map)*
10. Columbus read the _____ of Marco Polo. *(tale)*

LEARNING THE LANGUAGE

Belonging to Someone

When we want to show that a thing belongs to someone, we add a " ' " mark to the word. This mark is called an "apostrophe." Then we add an "s" to the apostrophe.

Example: The book of Jane was good.
Jane's book was good.

Add 's to each word to show "belonging to someone."

1. _____ crew was happy. *(Balboa)*
2. The _____ food was almost gone. *(crew)*
3. The _____ sail was white. *(ship)*
4. Did you see the _____ compass? *(captain)*
5. The _____ face was painted. *(Indian)*
6. The _____ cover was torn. *(book)*
7. Queen _____ money helped Columbus. *(Isabella)*
8. _____ explorers were good sailors. *(Spain)*
9. The _____ job was interesting. *(man)*
10. The Atlantic _____ waves were huge. *(Ocean)*

2

Colonies in America

KEY WORDS

settlement   A group of buildings in a new land. The first Europeans to come to America built *settlements*.

colony   Land that is owned and run by another country. Our land used to be a *colony* of England.

colonist   A person who lives in a colony. Henry Smith left England to live in the New World. Henry was a *colonist*.

apprentice   A young person who learned a trade by working with experts. Benjamin Franklin was an *apprentice* printer. That is how he learned to be a printer.

goods   Things made to be sold. Colonists made *goods* to sell to others.

manufacture   To make things in factories using machinery. The colonists *manufactured* goods to sell.

plantation   A huge farm that usually has one main crop. Most southern *plantations* grew tobacco. Later cotton was the main crop.

tutor   A private teacher. John and Mary lived in a large plantation in the South. They had a *tutor* to teach them their school work.

Spanish Colonies

The Spanish came to the New World for gold, God, and glory. They wanted to find gold and become rich. They also wanted to convert the Indians to the Catholic religion. And they wanted to be "big" men in their native country. Few wanted to stay in the New World. They wanted to get rich and go back to their "mother country."

Most of the Spaniards that stayed were Catholic *missionaries*. A missionary is a priest or minister who wants to convert others to his religion. The Spanish missions were places to teach Indians the Catholic religion. Spain set up many missions in their colonies.

England and France wanted colonies, too. The race was on! Each country wanted land in the New World.

FILL IN THE RIGHT ANSWER

1. Some Spanish people came to the New World for _____.
2. They set up _____ in the New World.
3. These people were called _____.
4. The colonists wanted to go back to _____.
5. They wanted to be _____ in Spain.
6. Spain was their _____ country.
7. The _____ religion was the official religion of Spain.
8. _____ taught Indians the Catholic religion.
9. England and _____ wanted _____ too.
10. They wanted _____ in the New World.

French Colonies

France was slow to set up colonies in the New World. Let us read this "pretend" newspaper to see why.

French Times

May 12, 1600   Price **5 Sous**

Colonies in the New World

Many French people wonder why we did not set up colonies in the New World. We did not have enough money when we were fighting Spain.

Now we have colonies in Canada. Our main business is furs. But killing the animals for their fur is dangerous.

Our fur trappers always make friends with the Indians. These trappers even learn the Indians' languages. But only a few trappers can make a living.

We only let a few rich people own land in the New World. We do not want a lot of our people to stay in the colonies.

FILL IN THE RIGHT ANSWER

Read the newspaper for the answers.

1. The French king did not have enough money for colonies. France needed its money for the _____ with Spain.
2. The main business of the French colonists was _____.
3. Killing the animals was _____ work.
4. The fur trappers learn the Indians' _____.
5. The French king did not want a lot of French _____ to stay in the colonies.

29

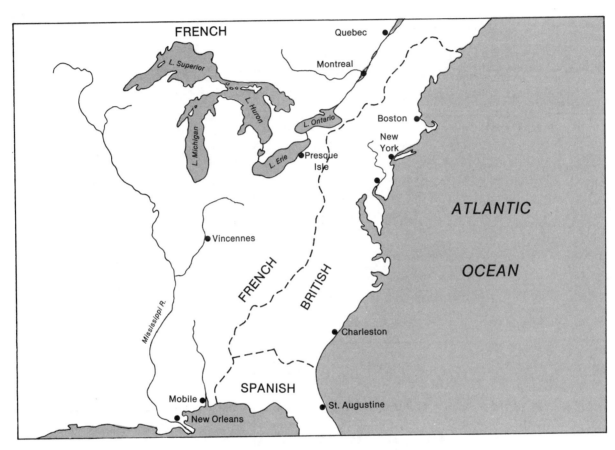

The French Colonies (1750)

English colonies were divided into three parts—New England, middle colonies, and southern colonies. Life in each type of colony was different.

JAMESTOWN—THE FIRST ENGLISH COLONY

The first English colonists left England in December, 1606. They did not reach the New World until April, 1607.

These colonists found a large river and named it the James River. It was named after their king—King James. On the shores of the river the colonists built a settlement. They called the new settlement "Jamestown."

In 1608, Captain John Smith was the leader of the colony. He was a good leader and made the people work together. John Smith also made friends with the Indians. The Indians gave the colonists food.

Captain Smith loved to explore. Some people say that unfriendly Indians captured Smith when he was exploring. His life was saved by the chief's daughter. Her name was Pocahontas.

WHICH WORD FITS?

Read these words. Most are from the story. Pick the word that fits the sentence. Be careful, there are extra words.

explore	**cook**	**swim**
king	**ship**	**river**
colonists	**leader**	**Jamestown**

1. The first English _____ left England in December, 1606.
2. The colonists named their first colony _____.
3. They named the colony and a nearby river after their _____.
4. John Smith became the _____ of the colony in 1608.
5. John Smith loved to _____.

John Smith and Map of New England

WHY ENGLISH PEOPLE CAME TO THE NEW WORLD

More people came to the New World from England than from Spain or France. Many English farmers were poor in the early 1600s. Their landlords wanted to use all of the farm land to raise sheep. The landlords got a lot of money for wool that came from the sheep. But the farmers did not have land to plant their crops. So many English farmers wanted to try the New World. They could own their own land in the New World. Then they could plant what they wanted.

Until 1603 English people had many more rights than other Europeans. But they got a new king in 1603. His name was King James. He took away much of their freedom. Rights the English had for hundreds of years were taken away. Many English people missed these rights. The New World gave them freedom.

Other English people came for religious reasons. The English king wanted everybody to belong to the same church. This church was the Church of England. But many people did not want to belong to this church. The New World gave them freedom to worship.

FILL IN THE CORRECT ANSWER

1. More people came to the New World from _____ than from Spain or France. (*Estonia, England*)
2. Most English farmers were _____ (*poor, part*) in the early 1600's.
3. Their landlords wanted to raise _____ (*sheep, shells*) for their wool.
4. The farmers did not have _____ (*lambs, land*) to plant their crops.
5. Until 1603 English people had more _____ (*writes, rights*) than other Europeans.
6. King James took away much of their _____ (*fools, freedom*).
7. The English king wanted everybody to belong to the same _____. (*church, chair*)
8. The New World gave people freedom to _____ (*wonder, worship*).

WHICH WORD FITS?

Choose the right word.

Pilgrims were people who came to the New World for freedom of religion. They came across the ocean on a _____ (*shape, ship*) called the "May-flower." The trip took over two months on a rough _____ (*sea, see*).

The Pilgrims set up a new colony. They called it Plymouth _____ (*Cow, Colony*). The Indians were very friendly. The Indians showed the colonists how to grow _____ (*tools, food*). In November, 1621, the colonists had their first Thanksgiving dinner. They shared their food with the _____ (*Insects, Indians*).

Puritans also came to the New World for religious freedom. They came to the _____ (*New World, New Jersey*) in 1628. The Puritans came to what is now the _____ (*state, country*) of Massachusetts.

The Puritans wanted everybody to worship as they did. They were very strict. Everybody had to pay for the church. People could not _____ (*argue, arrest*) with the leaders of the church. They came to the colonies for _____ (*religious, relative*) freedom. But they did not let people disagree with their church.

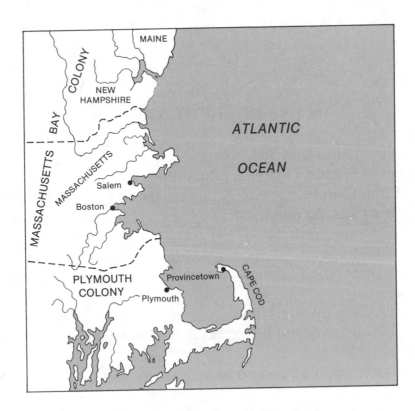

The Plymouth and Massachusetts Bay Settlements

ENGLISH COLONIES

The New England Colonies

The New England colonies were Massachusetts, New Hampshire, Connecticut, and Rhode Island. Today they are states.

New England had poor soil. The weather was bad for farming. There were many farmers. But they only grew food for themselves. They could not make money farming. The family needed all of the food they grew.

Fishing was good in New England. Fishing brought cash. Many people earned their living by trading. They traded with England. They sent fish and lumber to England. England sent goods to New England. New England needed ships for this trading. Ship-building was very important. This gave people many jobs.

The colonists began to manufacture goods. Manufacture means making goods. At first, goods were made in the home. Later, factories were set up. Factories were built near waterfalls. They used the water for power.

Most people in New England were Puritans. The Bible was their law. They worked hard and were honest people. Some people did not agree with the Puritans. They wanted religious freedom. These people moved from Massachusetts to their own colony. It is called Rhode Island.

The New England people believed in education. They set up public schools. They started the first college in North America. Its name is Harvard. Today, it is famous all over the world.

Many families wanted their children to learn a trade. The children became "apprentices." Apprentices learned trades by working with experts. This was another kind of schooling. After some years the apprentices became masters at their trades. Then, they could have apprentices help them.

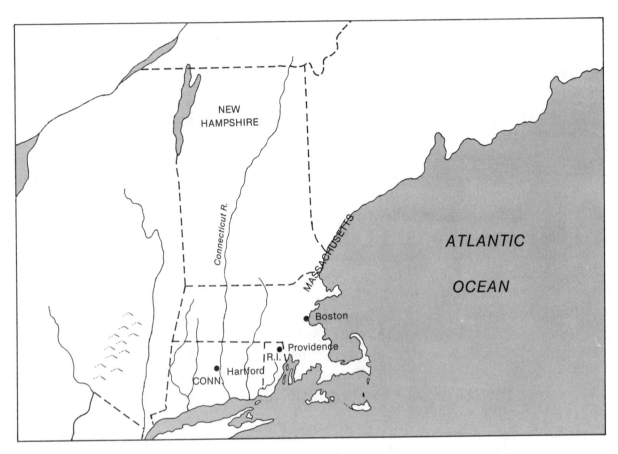

The New England Colonies

The Middle Colonies

The middle colonies were New York, New Jersey, Pennsylvania, and Delaware.

There were many farmers in the middle colonies. They grew more crops than in New England. The weather and soil of the middle colonies were better than in New England.

The middle colonies also had manufacturing. As in New England, it started in people's homes and later moved to factories. In the middle colonies, clothing, glass, and iron were important products.

People came from different places to the middle colonies. They came from England, Germany, Holland, France, and other countries. This was very different from New England. Most of the people in New England were from "old" England. They were mainly Puritans. In New York, people came from Holland, France, and "old" England too. Pennsylvania had people from England and Germany. They were of different religions.

People in the middle colonies had more freedom than in New England. In New England, a person had to be a Puritan. But in the middle colonies, people had the freedom to go to any church.

Massachusetts Bay Colonists

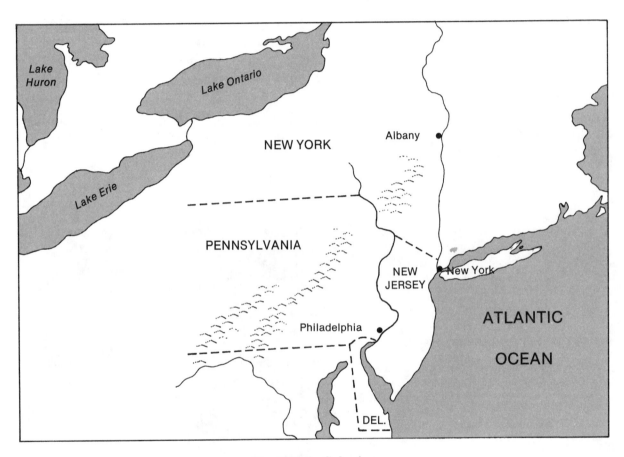

The Middle Colonies

Southern Colonies

The southern colonies were Virginia, Maryland, North Carolina, South Carolina, and Georgia. Most of the people in these colonies came from England. But they were not Puritans.

Nature was very kind to the southern colonies. These colonies had good weather all year. The growing season was longer here than in the other colonies. The soil was richer than in the northern colonies. There were many rivers and harbors in the South.

Large farms started in the southern colonies. These farms were called "plantations." Tobacco was the big cash crop. But it was hard work to grow tobacco. Each plantation needed many workers.

To get the work done, a cruel thing was done. This was to have slavery. Slavery is not an American idea or a southern idea. It was not a new idea. Slaves were used all over the world. There was slavery in Africa. The Arabs used slaves for many years before America was discovered. In Europe, white people called "serfs" were slaves to their white masters.

Plantation owners began to use slaves to help on the farms. These black slaves were taken from their homes in Africa. In the beginning the plantation owner sometimes worked with the slaves in the fields. But the slaves did most of the hard work. Some plantation owners became very rich. They had an "overseer" watch over the slaves. Sometimes the "overseer" was very cruel.

The southern colonies did not have many schools. Teachers came to the plantations to teach the white children. Each plantation had its own teacher. These teachers were called "tutors." Boys went to school longer than girls. Many rich boys went to school in England.

FILL IN THE RIGHT ANSWER

Choose the correct answer.

Write *NE* for New England colonies.
**   *MC* for middle colonies.**
**   *SC* for southern colonies.**

1. The _____ had the best climate and soil for farming.
2. The _____ used water power for many of their factories.
3. Plantations were common in the _____.
4. The _____ had people from many different countries.
5. The first college was started in the _____.
6. The _____ had tutors.
7. The smallest farms were in the _____.
8. Slaves were used in the _____.
9. The _____ did not have religious freedom.
10. The _____ had most of the apprentices.

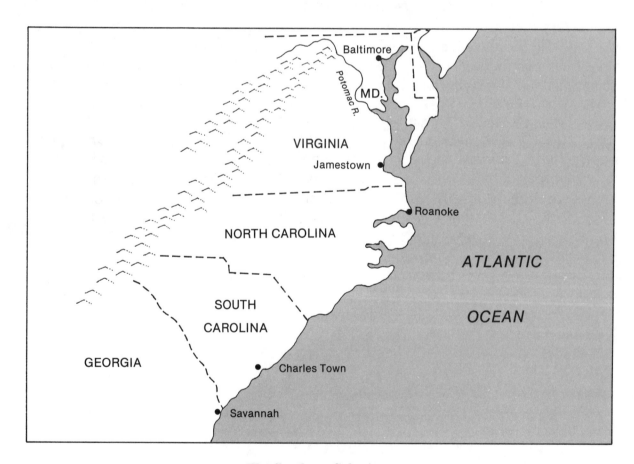

The Southern Colonies

WHICH WORD FITS?

Choose the correct word.

France and England ran their _____ (*colleges, colonies*) differently. French colonists did not want to stay. French farmers were happy in _____ (*France, Forts*). They did not want to live in the New World. Almost all French colonists killed _____ (*almonds, animals*) for their furs. They came to get rich. Then they wanted to go back to France.

France had much more _____ (*lend, land*) in the New World than England had. But they had few _____ (*people, ponies*) on the land. The French _____ (*Kind, King*) ran everything in the French colonies. The French colonists could not vote.

The French colonists were kind to the Indians. They traded with the _____ (*Indians, Indies*). The French colonists learned the Indians' _____ (*laps, languages*). They did not tear up the Indians' lands for farms.

Most English colonists came to the New World to stay there. In England, farm lands were used to raise _____ (*sheep, shammies*). Many English farmers came to the New World to _____ (*start, stay*) farms. Here was a chance to make a new life.

The English colonists had more rights and freedoms. English colonies grew fast. The English colonists did not have as much _____ (*land, legs*) as the French colonists. But the English colonists had more people. So they had many more _____ (*towns, tests*) than the French colonists.

The Indians did not like the English colonists. The English colonists _____ (*tore, told*) down trees. They cleared the land for farming. They spoiled the Indians' _____ (*heavy, hunting*) grounds. They treated the Indians as enemies.

The _____ (*Fans, French*) wanted to get rid of the English. So did the _____ (*Indians, Indents*).

41

LEARNING THE LANGUAGE

WHEN DID IT HAPPEN?

Present tense = now or today

Example:

    Present Tense
Spain *fights* with France.

Past tense = before now

    Past Tense
Spain *fought* with France.

Fill in the right tense:

1. Columbus _____ America.

   Columbus _____ America in 1492.

   (discovered, discovers)

2. They _____ the natives "Indians."

   They _____ the natives "Indians" when they landed.

   (call, called)

3. The French _____ in Canada.

   The French _____ in Canada when they set up colonies.

   (settled, settle)

4. English farmers _____ poor now.

   English farmers _____ poor in colonial times.

   (were, are)

5. The English people _____ much freedom today.

   The English people _____ much freedom until King James was king.

   (have, had)

6. We _____ history in school.

   The colonists' children _____ history.

   (studied, study)

LEARNING THE LANGUAGE
STATEMENTS AND QUESTIONS

Example: Question – Were English and French colonies different?
Statement – English and French colonies were different.

A *question* ends with a question mark – "?"
A *statement* ends with a period – "."

Change each question into a statement.

1. **Question** – Did English colonists want to stay in the New World?
   Statement –
2. **Question** – Were French farmers happy in France?
   Statement –
3. **Question** – Did French colonists trade furs?
   Statement –
4. **Question** – Did English colonies have more people?
   Statement –
5. **Question** – Were most French colonists kind to the Indians?
   Statement –

Change each statement into a question.

6. **Statement** – French colonists learned the Indians' languages.
   Question –
7. **Statement** – Most English colonists stayed in the New World.
   Question –
8. **Statement** – English colonists had more freedom.
   Question –
9. **Statement** – English colonies had more towns.
   Question –
10. **Statement** – The Indians liked the French colonists.
    Question –

43

FRANCE AND ENGLAND FIGHT OVER LAND

England and France wanted the same land in the New World. France built forts in the Ohio Valley. The English were angry when they saw these forts. The English colonists thought that this was their land.

This led to war. The French and Indians fought against the English. The English called this war the "French and Indian War."

English colonists helped the English army fight the French and Indians. Young George Washington was one of these colonists.

The war was very bloody. Many people were killed. The French lost. France lost its land in the New World. Now England and Spain owned all the land in North America.

FILL IN THE RIGHT ANSWER

Find these answers in the story.

1. England and France wanted the same _____. *(land, lend, laundry)*

2. France was in the _____ *(Hudson, Ohio, Pacific)* valley.

3. England thought the French were on their _____. *(hands, land, chair)*

4. The English started a _____ *(fire, riot, war)*.

5. The _____ *(English, French, Spanish)* were friendly with the Indians.

6. George Washington was a _____ *(English, French, Indian)* colonist who fought in the war.

7. The _____ *(English, French, Indians)* lost the war.

8. Now only _____ *(France and Spain, England and France, England and Spain)* had lands in the New World.

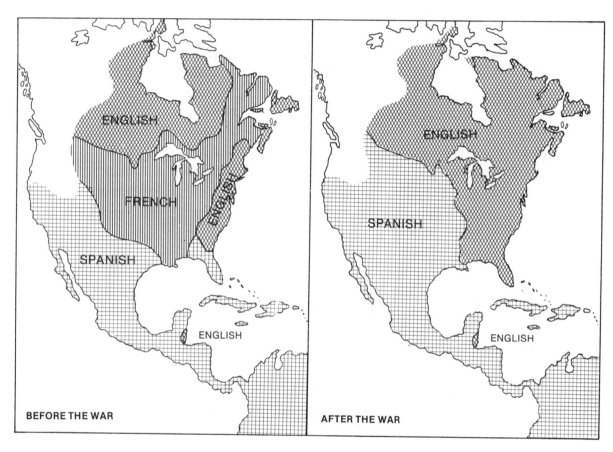

BEFORE THE WAR

AFTER THE WAR

**Boundaries Before and After the
French and Indian War**

45

LEARNING THE LANGUAGE

SYNONYMS

A *synonym* is a word that means almost the same as another word.
Example: happy   glad

Circle the synonym for each word.

Example	hot	(warm)	hard	cold
1. discover	run	find	jump
2. earth	world	Mars	sun
3. riches	stories	treasure	worries
4. idea	candy	concept	silly
5. exciting	dull	thrilling	thick
6. crazy	right	happy	foolish
7. believed	thought	laughed	lost
8. city	country	continent	town
9. fall	drop	fly	sleep
10. huge	many	big	small

TROUBLE BETWEEN ENGLAND AND THE COLONIES

There were thirteen English colonies. These colonies were loyal to England. Colonists wanted to obey the king of England. But they began to hate the way King George III treated them.

King George began to raise the colonists' taxes. England owed a lot of money. The king wanted the colonists to pay this money.

The colonists had to buy many things from England. They had to pay high prices. The colonists had to sell raw materials to England for low prices.

People who lived in England had a voice in government. Parliament was a group of people who helped the king pass laws. In England, people had members of Parliament to speak for them. The colonists didn't. The colonists did not have any "say" in the English government. But they had to pay high taxes. The taxes got higher and higher. More colonists became angry.

In those days, tea was the most important drink for English adults. The colonists had English habits. Most of them were born in England. Drinking tea was an English habit. Tea was very important to the colonists. Tea was like coffee is for Americans today.

When the king put a huge tax on tea, colonists started the famous Boston Tea Party. Colonists dressed up as Indians and quietly went on a ship in the Boston Harbor. They threw tons of tea overboard. This made King George very angry. He couldn't collect tax on the tea.

The Boston Tea Party

Newspapers Tell About the Boston Tea Party

Here is how stories about the Boston Tea Party might look in two newspapers.

London Times

December 16, 1773

Price **2 pence**

The Colonists Are Foolish

Many colonists sneaked on a ship in the Boston Harbor. They destroyed tons of good tea. This was very foolish. The tea was for the colonists.

The colonists are not good citizens. They do not want to pay their share of taxes. Colonists should pay more taxes than people who live in England. The colonies cost the king a lot of money.

The English government is working on new laws to punish the colonists for their mischief.

BOSTON NEWS

December 16, 1773

Price **3 pence**

Brave Men Fight High Taxes

Brave men showed King George that the colonists are tired of high taxes. These colonists dressed as Indians. They climbed aboard a ship in the Boston Harbor. These good men threw hundreds of pounds of tea into the sea.

We want to be loyal to the English government. But taxes are getting much too high. The King must lower our taxes. Colonists should have people in Parliament to help make laws.

The newspapers have different opinions on the Boston Tea Party.

Write "Times" after each statement that agrees with the *London Times*.
Write "News" after each statement that agrees with the *Boston News*.

1. The colonists' taxes are too high. _____
2. The Boston Tea Party was a good idea. _____
3. King George should lower taxes. _____
4. The colonists should have people in Parliament to help England make laws. _____
5. The colonists are not good citizens. _____

WRITE A LETTER

Sam Adams was a leader in Boston. He was very angry with the English. Help him finish this letter to a colonist in Virginia.

Boston, Massachusetts
February 2, 1774

George Washington
Mt. Vernon
Virginia

Dear George:

*By now you know about our _____ (**Brooklyn, Boston**) Tea Party on December 16, 1773. Do you remember the Boston Riot? Three years ago England sent hundreds of _____ (**silks, soldiers**) to Boston to keep order. A few children threw _____ (**snowballs, snacks**) at some English soldiers. The English soldiers fired _____ (**snakes, shots**) at the colonists. Five colonists died. The first to die was a Black. His _____ (**night, name**) was Crispus Attucks.*

*Many Boston citizens want to separate from _____ (**England, Germany**) to start their own _____ (**country, convention**). I agree with them. Please show this letter to the leaders in Virginia. Things are happening quickly. We may even have to fight England for our freedom. We need your help.*

Your servant,
Sam Adams

3

The American Revolution

KEY WORDS

delegate   A person who acts for or represents other people at a meeting or conference. Samuel Adams was elected to be a *delegate* at the meeting of the Continental Congress.

militia   A group of citizens that serves as a kind of part-time army for a colony or state. The citizens are not regular soldiers. The *militia* protected the town.

patriot   A person who loves his country and is loyal to it. *Patriots* thought of their colonies as their country. They wanted independence from the English king.

rebel   A person who fights against the government. Patrick Henry became a *rebel* against the English government.

treaty   An agreement between countries. The colonists signed a peace *treaty* to end the War of Independence.

THE COLONISTS' ANGER GROWS

The Boston Tea Party made some people in England very angry at the colonists. The English Parliament passed more laws to punish the colonies. One law said that colonists must let soldiers live in their homes. Another law took power away from Massachusetts. (Boston is a city in Massachusetts.)

The king wanted to punish Boston to teach the other colonies a lesson. But it did not work. The other colonies felt sorry for Boston. The cruel treatment made the colonies come together against the English.

A rebel is a person who fights against the government. Now there were many colonists who were rebels. Other colonists wanted to be loyal to England. Some didn't care who ran the government. They just wanted England to be fair with them.

On September 5, 1744, delegates from twelve colonies met at Philadelphia. They met to share ideas about their hard times with England. These colonists made a list of their troubles. It was a list of the rights that they wanted from England. This meeting was called the "First Continental Congress."

King George was angry when he heard about this meeting. The king thought that these colonists were traitors.

Each colony had a "militia." A militia is a group of civilians who are ready to defend the colony. It is like the National Guard of today. Now every town began to train its militia. War seemed sure.

Trouble started near Boston early in the morning of April 19, 1775. Paul Revere raced down the road on horseback shouting to the colonists that the British were coming. At Lexington, English soldiers ordered colonists to go home. The colonists refused. Shooting began. Eight colonists were killed and ten were wounded. Later that day, there was another battle at Concord. The English lost almost 300 men there.

FILL IN THE RIGHT ANSWER

Dec. 16 1773	Sept. 5 1774	April 19 1775
1.	2.	3.

Read the story and the letter to George Washington on Page 49. Tell what happened on each date on the time line.

1. _____

2. _____

3. _____

SOMETHING TO THINK ABOUT

What happened each time the king tried to punish the colonies?_____
_____
_____
_____
_____
_____

FIGHTING BEGINS

The Continental Congress met again in May, 1775. This was called the "Second Continental Congress." The delegates sent a letter to King George. The letter begged the king to treat the colonists fairly. The colonists knew that there might be a war. If they lost they would be hanged as traitors.

The king did not like the letter. Things got worse. Both sides were upset.

The Continental Congress was like a government. The Congress set up an army. They called the army the "Continental Army." The Congress looked for a soldier to lead the army. They picked Colonel George Washington. He had the most army experience.

A big battle was fought on June 17, 1775. It was called the Battle of Bunker Hill. About 15,000 colonists came to Boston. General Howe led the English Army. These were England's best soldiers. This was a big test for the colonists' army.

The colonists on Bunker Hill were short of gun powder. The colonists' army was told, "Don't fire until you see the whites of their eyes." This meant that they should hold their fire until the enemy got very close. They could not waste their gun powder.

The battle was very hard on both sides. But the Americans lost less men than the English! About 400 Americans were killed. But more than 1,000 English soldiers died.

This battle made the colonists proud. It showed that the American army could win over the mighty English army.

There were still some colonists who were loyal to the king. These colonists were called "Tories." Colonists who wanted to split from England were called "rebels" by the king.

But they called themselves "patriots."

George Washington

FILL IN THE RIGHT ANSWER

Find these answers in the story.

1. The Second Continental _____ (*Colonist, Congress*) met in May, 1775.
2. George Washington was picked to lead the _____ (*army, English navy*).
3. The _____ (*Battle, Bullet*) of Bunker Hill was fought on June 17, 1775.
4. Colonists were _____ (*sad, proud*) of their army after the Battle of Bunker Hill.
5. The colonists lost _____ (*more, less*) men than the British in the Battle of Bunker Hill.
6. Colonists who were loyal to the king were called _____. (*Tories, Stories*)
7. Colonists who wanted to split away from England were called _____ (*rebels, rifles*) by the king. They called themselves _____. (*patriots, traitors*)

THE DECLARATION OF INDEPENDENCE

The delegates to the Second Continental Congress knew that the king would not give them their rights. They decided to tell the world that they were free from England.

Thomas Jefferson was picked to write the paper. An important paper is called a document. This document is called the Declaration of Independence. It told why the colonists wanted freedom from England.

This was dangerous! Freedom could be gained only by war – a long and bloody war! If the colonists lost, they would be killed.

The Declaration of Independence was signed on July 4, 1776. That is our country's birthday.

The Declaration of Independence says that people have certain rights because they are human beings and that no one can take those rights away. The actual words are: "We hold these truths to be self-evident, that all men are created equal, that they are endowed by their Creator with certain unalienable Rights, that among these are Life, Liberty, and the pursuit of Happiness."

Some of the words in the Declaration need to be explained.

self-evident   obvious to everyone. It's *self-evident* that it's better to be free than a slave.

endowed   given as a gift. Some people are *endowed* with great talent.

unalienable   cannot be taken away. Today we spell this word **inalienable.** Her right to life, liberty, and happiness is *inalienable.*

The Declaration of Independence is one of the most famous documents in the world. It told the world why all people have rights.

The Signing of the Declaration of Independence

TRUE OR FALSE

Write *T* for each sentence that is true.
Write *F* for each sentence that is false

1. Thomas Jefferson wrote the Declaration of Independence. _____
2. The king of England signed the Declaration of Independence. _____
3. The Declaration of Independence said that all people have certain rights that no one can take away. _____
4. Most colonists wanted the king to take away their rights. _____
5. On July 4th we celebrate the signing of the Declaration of Independence. _____

MAKE A MATCH

Cause   Something that makes something else happen.
Effect   That which happens from a cause.

Example: *Cause:* I see a red light at the corner.
                    Effect: I stop my car.

Match the causes with the effects:

Cause

1. The English raise the colonists' taxes on tea. _____B_____
2. The colonists fight well at Bunker Hill._____
3. The king does not give the colonists their rights._____
4. The colonies need an army for protection._____
5. The colonists do not have enough gun powder._____

Effect

A. The colonists are told not to fire until they see the whites of their eyes.
B. The Boston Tea Party is held.
C. The Continental Army is set up.
D. The colonists want to separate from England.
E. The colonists are proud of their army.

LEARNING THE LANGUAGE
CONTRACTIONS

A *contraction* is a shorter word that is made from two words.

Example: *Don't* is the contraction for *do not*.

An apostrophe ' shows where the missing letters are.

Write the correct contraction in each sentence.

1. _____ (*Do not*) fire until you see the whites of their eyes."
2. The king _____ (*cannot*) see why the colonists are not happy.
3. _____ (*You are*) invited to the Boston Tea Party.
4. The king _____ (*does not*) want the colonists to fight.
5. General Washington _____ (*did not*) want to rest until the battle was over.
6. The colonists _____ (*have not*) asked for too much from the king.
7. _____ (*He will*) be here soon.
8. _____ (*I will*) be glad to see you.
9. _____ (*It is*) too late to stop the battle.
10. The king _____ (*should not*) be surprised that the colonists were angry.

FILL IN THE RIGHT ANSWER

Choose the right word.

The long war began. It was called the Revolutionary _____ (*War, Win*). It lasted for six years. The Americans fought for their freedom. They would lose certain rights if the English won.

The colonial army was very _____ (*week, weak*). It could not fight long battles with England. The American army suffered during the winter. The soldiers did not have enough _____ (*film, food*). Many American soldiers deserted.

The English army was better trained. They had more _____ (*guns, goats*). England hired soldiers from other countries to fight against the colonists. But the English had to fight on American land. They did not know the land as well as the Americans did.

Washington needed a victory. That would make his soldiers feel good. On December 25, 1776, General Washington's army crossed the Delaware River near Trenton, New Jersey. Washington picked Christmas Eve to _____ (*surprise, salute*) the enemy. It worked! The enemy soldiers were having a party. The Americans won. Only four Americans died.

Now, General Washington won more battles. He captured supplies that he needed badly. Washington soon won one of the most important _____ (*bats, battles*) of the war. The English held New York City. Washington fought bravely against a huge English army. He won New York back from the English.

But the fighting was not over. Washington camped at Valley Forge for the winter. It was a hard _____ (*waiter, winter*). The soldiers did not have enough supplies or clothes. The army did not have enough money. A trusted officer went over to the British side. His name was Benedict Arnold.

But the Americans had friends. Rich Americans loaned the country money. European countries helped the Americans. France was a big _____ (*heap, help*).

Many great _____ (*states, soldiers*) came from Europe to help the colonists. Marquis de Lafayette came from France. Baron Von Steuben came from Germany. Count Pulaski and T. Kosciusko came from Poland.

John Paul Jones won a bloody battle at sea. The English captain asked him to surrender. His answer is famous. He said, "I have not yet begun to fight." He fought on to _____ (*win, warn*) the battle.

The war went back and forth. The English army won many battles. But the last battle came on October 19, 1781. The English general, Cornwallis, moved his army into Virginia. General Cornwallis was trapped. He needed supplies. But the French fleet and American soldiers _____ (*traded, trapped*) him.

Now the English had to give up the war. The colonists beat the strongest _____ (*army, alarm*) in the world! They won their freedom from England. The new country was called the "United States." It had all the land between Canada and Florida, and all the land west to the Mississippi River.

A treaty is an agreement that is signed by different countries. The peace _____ (*tale, treaty*) for the Revolutionary War was not signed until September, 1783. The treaty was called the Treaty of Paris because it was signed in Paris, France.

The treaty told the world that a great new country was _____ (*bent, born*). The United States of America was now a free country.

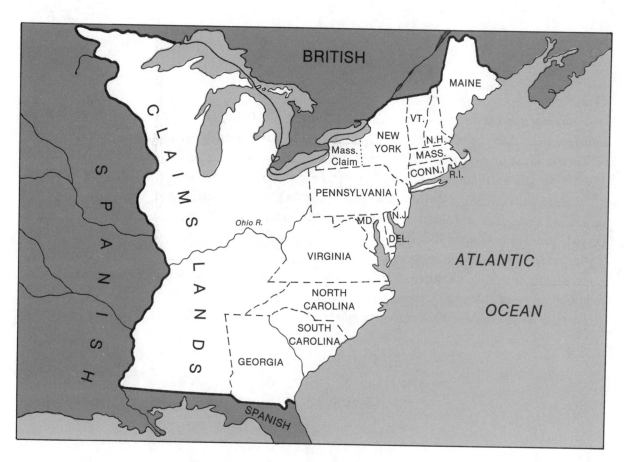

Boundaries of the United States (1783)

WRITE A LETTER

Pretend that a signer of the Treaty of Paris forgot to finish this letter to a friend. Finish the letter. Fill in the blanks with the right word.

Paris, France
September 3, 1783

Mr. Thomas Jones
New York

Dear Tom,
Today was a very exciting day. The _____ **(tale, treaty)** *was signed to end the Revolutionary War. Now I really feel* _____ **(independent, injured)** *from England.*
The war lasted so long. Many soldiers from both _____ **(signs, sides)** *died. General Washington deserves our thanks. One of the hardest parts of the war was the cold winter at* _____ **(Valley Forge, Vienna)**. *The soldiers had very little food and* _____ **(closing, clothing)**. *But most soldiers stayed* _____ **(loyal, lonely)** *to General Washington.*
Our side was lucky to get help from other _____ **(cities, countries)**. _____ **(France, Finland)** *was one of our best friends during the war. Great soldiers from Germany and Poland also helped us.*
I hope to see you in New York in about a month.

Your friend,
Benjamin Franklin

A NEW GOVERNMENT

People need *rules* to live together. A *government* makes rules and laws. These laws make the country fair to everyone.

The United States was a new country. It needed a new government to make life fair for its people.

The United States was made up of thirteen states after the war. The states did not agree on many things. They were like thirteen different countries.

The new country needed a constitution. A constitution is a plan for a government. It tells what kinds of laws may be passed.

Our new Constitution was called the Articles of Confederation. The states agreed to the new Constitution in 1781.

TRUE OR FALSE?

Write *T* for each sentence that is true.
Write *F* for each sentence that is false.

1. A government makes rules and laws. _____
2. The United States had twelve states after the war. _____
3. The states agreed on everything. _____
4. The new country needed a constitution. _____
5. A constitution is a plan for a government. _____
6. Our first constitution was the Declaration of Independence. _____
7. The states agreed to the new constitution in 1781. _____

THE ARTICLES OF CONFEDERATION

The Articles of Confederation was our first *constitution*. But the Articles of Confederation did not make the country strong. They made each state strong.

The people were afraid to make the new country too strong. They had a hard time under England. So, they did not trust a strong government for the country.

The country could not make the states pay taxes. They could only ask the states for money. The United States had trouble getting money to pay its bills.

The new country could not start an army to defend itself. It did not have courts. The Articles of Confederation did not let the country make treaties with other countries.

Each state was like a separate country. States were jealous of each other. The states had their own armies (militias). States printed their own money. People did not trust the states' money.

Leaders of the country saw that the Articles of Confederation did not work: the United States was not one country. The articles made the United States thirteen different countries. Other countries had trouble dealing with the United States.

The leaders knew that the Articles of Confederation must be changed! The country's government was too weak.

WHICH WORD FITS?

Read these words. Most are from the story. Pick the word that fits the sentence. There are extra words, so be careful.

weak	ships	Articles of Confederation
taxes	country	afraid
riches	money	changed

1. People were _____ to make the United States government too strong.
2. The _____ was our first constitution.
3. Each state was like a separate _____.
4. The United States could not make the states pay _____.
5. Each state printed its own _____.
6. The Articles of Confederation made the United States government too _____.

7. The country's leaders knew that the Articles of Confederation must be _____.

4

Making a New Nation

KEY WORDS

compromise   When people cannot agree — each gives up something so that both sides can get something more important. We had to *compromise* to pass the Constitution.

convention   A meeting for a special purpose. The doctors had a *convention* to learn about new medicines.

president   Somebody who runs a meeting or a country. The Constitutional Convention in Philadelphia picked George Washington to be its *president*.

representative   Somebody who acts or speaks for other people. A *representative* is like a delegate.

legislature   A group of representatives that makes laws. Your state *legislature* makes the laws of your state.

branch   A part of our government. Our government has three *branches*. They are the legislative, executive, and the judicial.

unconstitutional   A law that does not agree with the Constitution. The courts say that some laws are *unconstitutional*. These laws "die."

cabinet   People who help the president run his branch of the government. George Washington started the custom of picking a *cabinet* to help him.

electors   A few people chosen by the states to select a president. The 69 *electors* from the 13 states picked George Washington to be our first president.

power   The ability to do something. The president has the *power* to sign laws.

party   A group of people who share the same ideas on what the country does. Republicans and Democrats are now our two main *parties.*

term   The time that a person keeps his job. The president has a four year *term.*

A NEW CONSTITUTION

WHICH WORD FITS?

Choose the right word.

Delegates from twelve states _____ (*meat, met*) to fix the Articles of Confederation. Rhode Island was the only _____ (*state, spy*) that was not at the meeting. The meeting was held in Philadelphia in May, 1787.

An important meeting is called a convention. The delegates picked George Washington as president of the Convention.

The delegates saw that the Articles of Confederation did not work and could not be fixed. The country needed a new Constitution.

The _____ (*delegates, dealers*) wanted the new government to have three parts. These three parts were the LEGISLATIVE, EXECUTIVE, and JUDICIAL.

The LEGISLATIVE part of the _____ (*government, gown*) makes the laws. The EXECUTIVE _____ (*post, part*) of the government carries out the laws. The JUDICIAL part of the government runs the courts.

The delegates knew that the country's government must be _____ (*stolen, stronger*). But they did not agree on everything.

A compromise is a way of settling an argument. Each side gives up a little to get what they both want. What if you want to go to a baseball game but your friend wants to go to the movies? You can both go to the baseball game today and agree to go to the movies tomorrow.

A great compromise was made at the _____ (*court, convention*). There was an argument about the legislative branch of the government. Another name for the legislative branch is "Congress." The small states wanted each state to have the same number of representatives in the new Congress. The larger states wanted more representatives than the small states. This is because the larger states had more _____ (*people, pots*).

The leaders compromised. They made _____ (*two, to*) parts of the Congress. One part is the Senate. The Senate has two senators from each _____ (*steak, state*). The small states like the Senate because they have as much power as the larger states.

The larger states liked the other part of the compromise. The House of Representatives is the other part of Congress. Here the larger states have more representatives than the _____ (*smarter, smaller*) states.

Many other compromises were made because the states did not agree on everything. The Constitution was finished and signed in September, 1787. Now nine states had to _____ (*send, sign*) the Constitution to make it the new government.

Some people wanted to _____ (*sign, seek*) the Constitution as it was. These people were called "Federalists."

Other people were afraid the new Constitution gave the _____ (*government, gasoline*) too much power. They remembered their troubles with England. These people wanted more rights put in the Constitution. They were called "Anti-Federalists."

The people who wanted the Constitution signed made another _____ (*country, compromise*). They added a Bill of Rights to the Constitution. These are the first ten amendments to the Constitution. An amendment is something that fixes something or makes it better. The Bill of Rights gave us many new _____ (*writes, rights*). They help make our country a free country. We are free to do things that are not against the law.

CHECKS AND BALANCES

The people who wrote the Constitution were afraid of making the country's government too strong. That is why they made three parts in the new government. These parts are called branches.

Remember—each branch has its own job to do. The three branches share the power. One branch cannot get all the power.

The legislative branch is Congress and makes laws. The executive branch is the president, who enforces the laws. The judicial branch runs the courts.

But each branch can also stop another branch from doing things. The president usually must sign a bill that Congress passes before it can become law. Congress must agree with some things that the president does or wants done. The courts can rule laws unconstitutional.

FILL IN THE RIGHT ANSWER

Find these answers in the story.

1. The people who wrote the Constitution were afraid to make the new government too _____.
2. There are _____ parts to our country's government.
3. The _____ branch makes laws.
4. The _____ branch enforces the laws.
5. The _____ branch runs the courts.
6. Each branch has its own _____ to do.
7. Each branch can _____ another branch from doing things.
8. The _____ can rule laws unconstitutional.
9. The president must usually sign a _____ that Congress passes before it can become law.
10. Congress must _____ with some things that the president does or wants done.

LEARNING THE LANGUAGE
HOMONYMS

A *homonym* is a word that sounds the same as another word. The words are spelled differently. They also have different meanings.

Example: **deer**   **dear**

Circle the *homonym* for each word.

Example	**sail**	**soft**	**sale**	**send**
1. beat	beet	best	both
2. two	ten	to	tall
3. eight	ate	act	ant
4. sun	snake	son	silly
5. pear	pull	post	pair
6. know	new	no	now
7. knew	net	new	not
8. knot	next	not	note
9. week	well	weak	wall
10. would	wood	want	went

THE NEW GOVERNMENT WORKS

The new Constitution was good. It made the country's government strong. But it did not give power to one group. The country also shared some powers with the states.

Now, the United States was really one country. It was not like thirteen separate countries any more. The United States could now deal with other countries. The money system was better. The states were not as jealous of each other.

The President (Executive Branch)

Each state chose electors to pick the president. They picked George Washington for president. John Adams was the vice-president.

George Washington was our first president. He knew that he must do a good job because future presidents would copy things that he did. His actions set the standard for the new government.

Washington made departments to help him run the country. The heads of these departments became his cabinet. Later, other presidents did the same. They also had cabinets to help them run the government.

Congress (Legislative Branch)

The legislative branch of government has two parts. These are the Senate and the House of Representatives. Each state has two senators in the Senate. Larger states have more members in the House of Representatives than smaller states. So, all states do not have the same number of representatives.

Each senator serves six years in Congress. In the beginning, senators were chosen by state legislators. The people voted directly only for members of the House of Representatives. Representatives serve only two years and then have to run in an election if they want to be in Congress again. Later, both senators and representatives were chosen directly by the people.

The Courts (Judicial Branch)

The country's court system also was created. The lowest court is the District Court. The Courts of Appeals are higher. People who lost their cases in the District Court got another chance in the Court of Appeals. The Supreme Court is the highest court in the country. It has the "last word." The Supreme Court also decides whether laws are OK according to the Constitution.

WHICH WORD FITS?

Read these words. Most of them are from the story. Pick the word that fits the sentence. There are extra words.

cabinet	strong	electors
copy	election	Court of Appeals
country	District	Supreme

1. The new Constitution made the country's government _____.
2. Now the United States was really one _____.
3. Each state chose _____ to pick the president.
4. George Washington knew that future presidents would _____ things he did.
5. George Washington picked a _____ to help him run the country.
6. The lowest court in the United States is the _____ Court.
7. The _____ is the next highest court.
8. The highest court in the United States is the _____ Court.

Fill in the right words in this newspaper. It was printed at the end of President Washington's term. The newspaper tells about his goodbye speech to the country. It is called his "Farewell Address." It is a famous speech.

Washington News

February 20, 1797

Price **3 Cents**

Washington Says Goodbye!

George Washington gave his last speech as our _____ (lawyer, president). It is called his Farewell Address.

We are _____ (patient, proud) of our first president. His speech showed how great he is. The _____ (speech, radio) said that Americans should always think of the whole country. He said that the Constitution was made by the _____ (people, kings). All people should _____ (obey, forget) the Constitution.

President Washington told how all parts of the country are _____ (injured, important). He showed that the government helped all parts of our great country.

George Washington said that we should be careful of _____ (final, foreign) countries. He did not want us to get mixed up in other countries' fights.

Washington could have been _____ (elected, erected) as president again. He thought that eight _____ (years, weeks) as president was enough. The United States will never forget his work for our country. We wish him good health and happiness.

LEARNING THE LANGUAGE
BASE WORDS

We use *base words* with different endings to make new words.

Base Word	New Words	
independent	independence	independently
revolt	revolution	revolutionary
colony	colonist	colonial
represent	representation	representative

Use one of the word forms in each sentence.

1. We were a _____ of England.

2. The English _____ government was unfair to the colonists.

3. The _____ fought The Revolutionary War to be _____ of England.

4. Sometimes the Revolutionary War was called the War for _____.

5. American colonists did not have a _____ to speak for them in the English government.

6. They were taxes with anyone to _____ their point of view.

7. After the Revolution, the Americans had _____ in the Congress.

LEADERS DO NOT AGREE

John Adams was our second president. He became president in 1797. Most Americans liked President Washington. But not everyone liked John Adams.

Presidents keep their jobs for four years. Then they must "run" again for another four year term. John Adams did not win another term. Thomas Jefferson beat him in 1800.

Americans did not agree on how the country should run. That is why there were different parties. John Adams belonged to the Federalist party. Alexander Hamilton was also a Federalist leader. Hamilton was President Washington's Secretary of the Treasury. He thought that rich and educated people should govern the country. He wanted to build many factories to make the country strong.

Thomas Jefferson was the leader of the Anti-Federalists who were now called the Democratic-Republicans or Republicans for short. Republicans thought that the average person could govern the country.

Jefferson was our third president. He thought that all of the people should be able to read and write. Free public schools were the way to make this possible, he said. He also thought that people have a right to their opinions and that the right to be wrong must be protected.

TRUE OR FALSE?

Read the story.
Write *T* if the statement is true.
Write *F* if the statement is false.
Example: Thomas Jefferson was our third president. _____T_____

1. John Adams won the election of 1800. _____
2. All Americans agree on how the government should be run. _____
3. Federalists believed that ordinary people should run the government. _____
4. Thomas Jefferson believed that ordinary people could run the goverment. _____
5. Presidents keep their jobs for six years. _____
6. Thomas Jefferson wanted free public schools. _____

ELECTION NOTICE

VOTE FOR THOMAS JEFFERSON
FOR PRESIDENT!

VOTE AGAINST THE FEDERALISTS!
TOM JEFFERSON CARES ABOUT YOU!

JEFFERSON IS FOR THE PEOPLE!
JEFFERSON IS FOR PUBLIC SCHOOLS!
LET THE PEOPLE RUN THE COUNTRY!

MAKE YOUR VOTE COUNT . . .
DON'T VOTE FOR ADAMS!

WHICH WORD FITS?

Read these words. Some are from the election poster. Pick the word that fits the sentence. Make your choice carefully. There are extra words.

facts	Adams	Jefferson
Republicans	opinions	ad
television	money	Federalist

1. This poster tells us to vote for _____.
2. The poster is like an _____ in a newspaper.
3. Today we have commercials on _____ asking us to vote for people.
4. This poster tells the _____ of people who want Jefferson to be the president.
5. The sign tells us not to vote for the _____ party.

MAKE A MATCH

Write the letter that tells what each person did next to the name that fits. The first one is done for you.

1. Alexander Hamilton___G___
2. Marquis de Lafayette_____
3. Thomas Jefferson_____
4. Samuel Adams_____
5. Baron Von Steuben_____
6. George Washington_____
7. General Cornwallis_____
8. Count Pulaski_____
9. Christopher Columbus_____
10. Marco Polo_____

A. The third president of the United States. He wrote the Declaration of Independence.

B. His stories gave Christopher Columbus the idea to explore.

C. German general who helped colonists win their independence from England.

D. The second president of the United States.

E. Came from Poland to help colonists win their independence from England.

F. Discovered New World.

G. Washington's Secretary of the Treasury

H. First president of the United States.

I. Came from France to help colonists win their independence from England.

J. English general who was trapped by General George Washington.

FILL IN THE RIGHT ANSWER

Choose the right word.

Thomas Jefferson bought a huge amount of _____ (*land, sand*) in 1803. He _____ (*sent, bought*) this land from France. This was called the Louisiana Purchase. It doubled the size of the United States. Now the United States went all the way _____ (*east, west*) as far as the Rocky Mountains. It went from Canada to the Gulf of Mexico.

In 1819 the United States _____ (*bought, brought*) Florida from Spain. Americans were _____ (*proud, pound*) of their country's growth. Now many Americans went west to find _____ (*land, literature*). They wanted to own their own farms. They were pioneers. They faced many _____ (*dangers, dancers*). They had to go into _____ (*Insurance, Indian*) land. Travel was hard.

New states came into the United States. The United States was _____ (*growling, growing*) fast. It was becoming a _____ (*big, baseball*) country.

Other _____ (*countries, cities*) respected the United States. People from other countries came to the United States. Some of these people came to get _____ (*lost, rich*) here. Many other people came to find _____ (*free, freedom*).

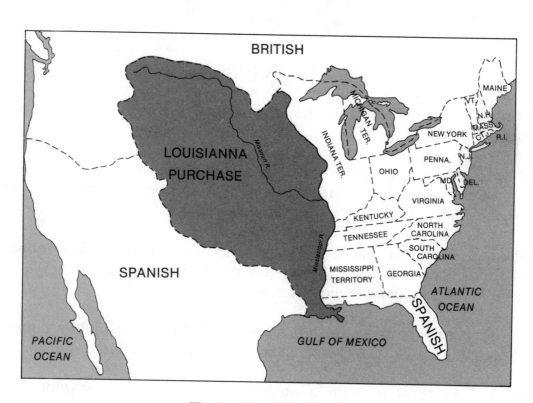

The Louisiana Purchase

5

The Growing Pains of a Young Nation

KEY WORDS

foreigner   One who lives in another country. John lives in England. John is a *foreigner*.

patent   Protection for someone who invents something. The Constitution ordered Congress to make *patent* laws. This encouraged inventors. Nobody could copy their inventions to make money.

revolution   A sudden and complete change in something. The Industrial *Revolution* changed the way things were made. The *Revolutionary* War gave the United States independence from England.

profit   The amount of money left after the cost of something in business. John bought a watch for $10 and sold it for $15. He made a *profit* of $5.

profitable   Worthwhile from a business point of view. Growing cotton became *profitable* after the cotton gin was invented.

Congress   The part of the government that makes laws: the Senate and House of Representatives. Each state has people in *Congress* who look out for their needs.

foreign   Any country besides the United States. France is a *foreign* country.

northerner   A person who lives in the North. Many *northerners* did not like slavery.

southerner   A person who lives in the South. Many *southerners* had slaves on their plantations.

tariff   A special tax on goods made in another country. The tax is charged when the goods are brought into this country. This makes the goods more expensive. It protects American factories and workers. The workers wanted a *tariff* on English goods.

westerner   A person who lives in the West. *Westerners* wanted cheap land and better roads

dictator   A ruler who has complete power in his country. Hitler was a *dictator* in Germany.

independence   freedom. The United States won its *independence* from England in 1776.

territory   Land ruled by a country. Oklahoma was a *territory* of the United States before it was a state.

THE INDUSTRIAL REVOLUTION

The United States makes many things today. American goods are sold all over the world. These things are made in factories. But we did not always have factories.

People used to make things by hand in their homes. Families made their own clothing. Farmers made their own tools.

The Industrial Revolution changed the way people made things. It was a sudden change. That is why it is called a "revolution."

The Industrial Revolution started in England. In 1764, a man invented a machine to make thread from wool. This does not seem so great today. But it was an amazing thing in 1764. The machine was run by hand.

Soon people made the machine better. People began using water power for the machine. Other machines were invented. A machine was invented to weave cloth. This was a power loom. People used hand looms before this invention. The machine was much faster than hand looms.

These machines helped England sell material all over the world. England could make good material cheaply. Other countries could not match the prices or quality. This made England a mighty country.

England passed laws to stop people from selling machines to foreigners. Many people from other countries tried to get these machines. At first, they had no luck. No machines left England.

Samuel Slater was an Englishman who knew machines. He wanted to come to the United States with his machines. Slater had to sneak out of England. He grew a long beard.

It worked! Slater came to the United States. He worked hard to make a machine to make cotton yarn. In 1790 Slater finished his machine. This machine helped the United States join the Industrial Revolution.

The machine could use huge amounts of cotton to make material. But a factory could not get enough cotton. Cotton was very expensive in 1790.

Eli Whitney came to the rescue! He invented the cotton gin in 1793. The cotton gin easily separated the cotton from its seeds and dirt. This made the cotton profitable. Now huge amounts of cotton could be grown in the South.

The steam engine also was an important invention. It was patented in 1769 by James Watt. Steam engines were used in factories. Without steam engines there might not have been an Industrial Revolution.

Later, steam engines were used for trains and steamships. In 1803, Robert Fulton of Philadelphia invented the steamship. And in 1814 the first steam-powered locomotive was built in England.

A Great Invention

Eli Whitney is a teacher in Georgia. Whitney invented a great machine last year. His "cotton engine" makes cotton profitable to grow. People are calling it "cotton gin" for short.

One cotton gin can clean as much cotton as twelve people. Tobacco is no longer the South's most important crop. Tobacco farmers can now grow cotton instead. Tobacco is hard on the land. It ruins the soil. By growing cotton, farmers will make more money. Their land will not be spoiled.

Cotton gins are spreading all over the South. Now, cotton plantations are getting bigger. The larger plantations need more slaves. Cotton is becoming so important in the South that people call it "King Cotton."

WHICH WORD FITS?

Read the newspaper. Choose the right word.

1. Eli Whitney was a _____ in Georgia.

     a. teacher   c. trader
     b. tailor   d. trucker

2. The cotton gin was first called a cotton _____.

     a. seeder   c. engine
     b. puller   d. picker

3. One cotton gin can clean as much cotton as _____ people.

     a. two   c. six
     b. ten   d. twelve

4. The cotton gin made cotton _____ to grow.

     a. more costly   c. harder
     b. impossible   d. profitable

5. Plantations became _____ because of the cotton gin.

       a. fewer   c. poor

       b. cheaper   d. larger

6. _____ was the most important crop in the South before the invention of the cotton gin.

       a. Coffee   c. Tobacco

       b. Wheat   d. Corn

7. Tobacco _____ the land.

       a. cleans   c. feeds

       b. spoils   d. smokes

8. As plantations grew larger, they used more _____.

       a. slaves   c. books

       b. northerners   d. tobacco

9. Cotton gins _____ all over the South.

       a. spread   c. walked

       b. spilled   d. crawled

10. People called cotton "King Cotton' because it was so important to the _____.

       a. North   c. South

       b. East   d. West

TRUE OR FALSE

Read the story .
Write *T* if the statement is true.
Write *F* if the statement is false.

Example: England was the first country to have factories. _____T_____

1. Revolution means a slow change in something. _____
2. The first machines were worked by hand. _____
3. England's machines let it sell good material at low prices _____
4. England shared its machines with the rest of the world. _____
5. Samuel Slater made the first American machine. _____
6. Cotton was very expensive in 1790. _____
7. The cotton gin made cotton too expensive. _____
8. The first cotton gin was made in the United States. _____
9. A patent protects inventors by not letting other people copy their inventions. _____
10. The United States started the Industrial Revolution. _____

MAKE A MATCH

Choose the correct letter. The first one is done for you.

1. cotton gin __E__
2. patent _____
3. national government_____
4. independent _____
5. Tory _____
6. electors _____
7. foreigner _____
8. loom _____
9. revolution _____
10. Industrial Revolution _____

A. A sudden change in something.
B. People who choose a president.
C. The sudden change in the way things were made.
D. Protection for someone who invents something.
E. A machine that cleans cotton. It made cotton profitable to grow.
F. The government of a country.
G. A machine for weaving cloth.
H. Free. Able to take care of yourself.
I. One who lives in another country.
J. A colonist who was loyal to the king of England.

ANOTHER WAR WITH ENGLAND

France and England were at war for many years. They started fighting while George Washington was president. President Washington said we would not choose sides. So the United States sold goods to both sides. The French and English did not like this.

Napoleon was the French leader. He warned the whole world not to trade with England. England warned all countries not to trade with France.

The French and English stopped many American ships. They stopped the ships to make sure that the United States was not trading with their enemy. Both France and England took some of our ships. President Jefferson complained to both countries, but they did not stop.

England made us more angry than France. The English began taking American sailors into their navy. They would stop American ships and take the sailors away. England said that these sailors were Englishmen. They were really American citizens.

The English navy had trouble getting men. This was because the officers were cruel. They whipped the sailors for small things. To get the men the English navy needed, the officers stole sailors from the American ships. This made the United States angry. Now the United States began to think of war with England.

The war began in June, 1812. That is why it is called the "War of 1812." The United States won more battles on the sea than on the land. The English attacked our coast and their army entered Washington, D.C. They burned the president's house and the Capitol building.

English ships sailed to Baltimore, Maryland. The English fired upon Fort McHenry all day and night. Francis Scott Key was an American. He watched the battle all night. The American flag was still flying over the fort in the morning. Key was so happy that he wrote a poem that became the Star Spangled Banner.

The war ended in December, 1814. It was our last war against England. England and the United States are good friends now.

The Burning of Washington, D.C.

WHICH WORD FITS?

Choose the right word.

1. The United States had to fight a _____ war with England.

        a. safe   c. secret
        b. second   d. soldier

2. English ships took sailors from _____ ships and put them into the English navy.

        a. American   c. Indian
        b. French   d. German

3. The English army attacked _____. They burned the White House and the Capitol building there.

        a. Washington   c. New York
        b. Chicago   d. Boston

4. The _____ attacked Fort McHenry all night. The American flag was still flying in the morning.

        a. English   c. American
        b. French   d. German

5. Francis Scott Key saw the attack at Fort McHenry. He was _____ that the Americans won. He wrote the Star-Spangled Banner.

        a. sad   c. mad
        b. happy   d. sorry

TRUE OR FALSE?

Read the story.
Write *T* if the statement is true.
Write *F* if the statement is false.

Example: Napoleon was an English leader. _____ F _____

1. France and England were fighting when Washington was president. _____
2. The French and English stopped American ships. _____
3. France kidnapped sailors from American ships. _____
4. English navy officers were kind to their men. _____
5. War between England and the United States began in 1812. _____
6. This was the second war between England and the United States. _____
7. The United States won more battles on the land than on the sea. _____
8. The English army entered Washington, D.C. _____
9. Francis Scott Key was an English general. _____
10. England and the United States fought against each other after the War of 1812. _____

Newspapers and the War of 1812

Let us pretend that we have two newspapers that were printed before the War of 1812. One newspaper is English. The other newspaper is American. Each newspaper has different ideas on what caused the War of 1812.

Here is how the newspapers might look.

☆ ☆ ☆ American Eagle ☆ ☆ ☆

December 15, 1811

Price **3 Cents**

ENGLISH PIRATES KIDNAP AMERICAN SAILORS!

EXTRA! EXTRA! EXTRA!

English navy captains are kidnapping American sailors! These cowards pretend that the American sailors are really English. The sailors are American citizens. The English are no better than pirates.

English warships have been stopping our ships for years. The English say that they have to search our ships. They pretend to make sure that we do not trade with France. Americans have a right to trade with any country.

The United States will not stand for this kidnapping. If the English do not stop, war is certain. The English forgot who won the last war between our countries. We may have to remind them.

★ *English News* ★

December 15, 1811

Price **3 pence**

AMERICANS HIDE ENGLISH SAILORS!

EXTRA!   EXTRA!   EXTRA!

Americans hide many English sailors on American ships. These sailors were born in England. Americans say that they are American citizens. They are not! They are Englishmen! The Royal Navy needs these men. We have a right to take them. We are fighting a tough war with Napoleon of France.

We have other arguments with the United States. They sell goods to France. This makes it harder for us to fight the war with France.

The United States must stop helping France. They must also stop hiding our sailors. If they do not, we might have to teach them a lesson. We will go to war. This time, we are sure that England will win.

The *American Eagle* and the *English News* have different opinions.

FILL IN THE RIGHT ANSWER

Write "Eagle" after each statement that agrees with the *American Eagle*.
Write "News" after each statement that agrees with the *English News*.

1. The sailors on American ships are English. _____
2. The English are pirates. _____
3. The United States is helping France. _____
4. Americans have a right to trade with any country. _____
5. There might be a war between England and the United States. _____

LEARNING THE LANGUAGE
PREFIXES

A base word is the main part of a word. Prefixes are used before base words. The prefixes change the meaning of the base word. Some common prefixes are *un, dis, pre,* and *re*.

un and **dis** mean not.
re means again.
pre means before.

Tell what the underlined prefix means in these sentences.

Example: The English ship was <u>un</u>sure of its location._____not_____

1. The Americans <u>dis</u>agreed with the English navy.
    _____

2. The English wanted to make the seas <u>un</u>safe for ships trading with France.
    _____

3. Americans thought that the English were <u>dis</u>honest when they kidnapped American sailors. _____

4. The English captain <u>re</u>read his maps because he was lost. _____

5. The ship's compass was <u>pre</u>adjusted. _____

6. The sailor followed a <u>pre</u>set course. _____

7. The soldier <u>dis</u>mounted from his horse. _____

8. Let the captain sleep <u>un</u>disturbed. _____

9. Taking sailors off ships was <u>un</u>fair. _____

10. Americans finally <u>re</u>took the land the British occupied. _____

THE STATES ARGUE

The United States got stronger after the War of 1812. More people came to this country. Many of them went west. They wanted a new chance for a better life.

The United States had three main parts. These were the North, South, and West. The three parts did not agree on what the country should do.

The North had many factories. High tariffs helped American factories sell their goods. Tariffs made the price of foreign goods higher. Northerners wanted high tariffs. The South had many tobacco and cotton growers, and very few factories. Southerners did not want high tariffs. They wanted to buy things cheaply from other countries.

Southerners also wanted to sell their crops to other countries. High tariffs discouraged other countries from trading with the United States. Foreign businesses had to charge more for their goods and not make as much money. Southerners did not want to pay higher prices to help the northern factories. They wanted to buy cheap foreign goods.

Westerners needed roads and cheap land. They wanted the government to give them these things. Other parts of the country did not want to pay for the West. The northern factory owners were afraid. They thought their workers might head west if the land was too cheap.

Each part of the country had representatives in Congress. The representatives of each part of the country argued for their people.

TRUE OR FALSE?

Read the story.
Write _T_ if the statement is true.
Write _F_ is the statement is false.
Example: All parts of the United States agreed with each other. _____F_____

1. The North wanted a high tariff to protect its factories. _____
2. The South wanted a high tariff. _____
3. A high tariff makes goods cheaper. _____
4. The West wanted cheap land and roads. _____
5. The North wanted to help the West. _____
6. Each part of the country had representatives to look out for their needs.
   _____
7. The South had many factories. _____

ANDREW JACKSON

WHICH WORD FITS?

Choose the right word.

Andrew Jackson was our seventh _____ (_president, resident_). He was not like the other presidents. He was not as well educated. He was for the common people. But he was stubborn. He made many enemies.

President Jackson fired many government workers. He put his _____ (_friends, horses_) in these jobs. He _____ (_rewarded, lost_) his friends.

Westerners liked Jackson. He was from the West. He wanted them to have cheap roads. But he thought that each state should _____ (_pay, play_) for its own roads.

Jackson had to face a big problem. The South was getting _____ (_angry, happy_) about high tariffs. The tariffs made one of the southern states very angry. South Carolina said that it would leave the United States because of the high tariffs. Jackson said that no _____ (_country, state_) has the right to leave the United States. He was very strong and firm.

Congress made a _____ (_compromise, contest_) that settled the problem. They lowered the tariff. But the southern states were not completely happy. They thought that states should have more power.

LEARNING THE LANGUAGE
ANTONYMS

An *antonym* is a word that means the *opposite* of another word.
Example: slow   fast

Circle the antonym for each word.

Example	hot	warm	hard	(cold)
1. lose	discover	drop	catch
2. long	tall	short	fun
3. riches	junk	treasure	prize
4. round	red	flat	heavy
5. exciting	boring	thrilling	thick
6. happy	bright	silly	unhappy
7. float	swim	sink	run
8. peace	quiet	war	good
9. night	dark	week	day
10. huge	tiny	big	large

TEXAS AND MEXICO

Mexico is our southern neighbor. Mexico won its independence from Spain in 1821. People living in Texas, Arizona, and New Mexico became Mexican citizens.

Americans wanted to go to Texas. Most of the good land in the American West was gone. It was mostly desert. But, Texas had good land. The Americans wanted to settle there. Mexico let many Americans settle in Texas.

Mexico wanted to build up Texas. The Mexicans wanted a lot of people in Texas. They thought that would make Mexico stronger. But soon too many Americans came to Texas.

Texas Wins Its Independence

Mexico stopped new American settlers. A dictator ruled Mexico in 1834. His name was General Santa Anna. He said all Mexico, including Texas, had to obey him.

Santa Anna ordered that Americans stop coming into Texas. He also said that slavery will not be allowed in Mexico, including Texas. Most of the Americans in Texas owned slaves. They did not want to give up their slaves.

Mexico also collected taxes on goods brought in from the United States. Santa Anna made the Americans in Texas angry. Many Texan Americans thought Texas should stop being part of Mexico.

Texan Americans fought for independence from Mexico. They wanted Texas to be a separate country. Sam Houston was a good soldier. He became the leader of the Texas soldiers. Davy Crockett was a famous Indian fighter. He joined the Texas army.

The texas army tried to defend a mission church. It was called the "Alamo." The Mexican army ordered the Texans to leave the Alamo. The Texas army fired a cannon at the Mexicans. This started the battle. After a bloody battle, the Texans lost. All of the soldiers died. Now other Texans were angry. Hundreds of Texans joined to fight the Mexicans. "Remember the Alamo!" became a battle cry.

Texas became independent after much fighting. Texas was a separate country for nine years. Many people wanted Texas to join the United States. It did. Texas became a state in 1845.

The War with Mexico

Mexico started to argue about the boundaries of Texas. This led to fighting between American scouts and Mexican soldiers. The United States and Mexico went to war. The United States won the war. Now New Mexico and California were territories of the United States. The United States agreed to pay Mexico $15,000,000 for this land.

TRUE OR FALSE?

Read the story.
Write *T* if the statement is true.
Write *F* if the statement is false.

Example: Many Americans settled in Texas. _____T_____

1. Mexico is our northern neighbor. _____
2. Mexico let many Americans come in to build up Mexico. _____
3. After a while, Mexico thought that too many Americans came to Mexico. _____
4. Mexico never tried to stop Americans from coming to Mexico. _____
5. A dictator ruled Mexico in 1834. _____
6. Americans like dictators. _____
7. General Santa Anna allowed slavery in Mexico. _____
8. Texans fought to make Texas an independent country. _____
9. The United States lost the war with Mexico. _____
10. The United States got new land from the war with Mexico. _____

WHICH WORD FITS?

Choose the right word.

In 1848 gold was _____ (*discovered, lost*) in California. James Marshall was building a mill for John Sutter. Marshall found pieces of _____ (*gold, snow*) near the mill. The mill was near Sacramento, California. The news spread all over the country. By 1849, everybody wanted to come to California to find _____ (*gold, diamonds*).

Thousands of people rushed to California. This was called the "Gold Rush." Many came by _____ (*plane, wagon train*). Others came by ship.

Most people did not find gold. A few were lucky to find a little gold dust. Many families could not find a place to stay. Prices in California became very high. People had to find other jobs in order to live.

The Gold Rush brought many people to _____ (*Texas, California*) within a few years. It took _____ (*days, years*) for California to recover from the Gold Rush.

6

The Civil War

KEY WORDS

abolitionist   A person who wanted to stop slavery at once. Harriet Beecher Stowe was an *abolitionist*. She wrote a book against slavery. It was called *Uncle Tom's Cabin*.

planter   The owner of a plantation. Some *planters* owned many slaves.

Confederate States of America   The new country started by the South. *The Confederate States of America* picked Jefferson Davis to be its president.

Union   The United States. President Lincoln said that states could not leave the *Union*.

advantage   Something that helps a side to win. The North had more factories, railroads, and soldiers. These were *advantages* for the North.

blockade   A way to stop a country from selling or buying things from other countries. A "wall" of ships is put around the country to stop ships from going in or out. The North formed a *blockade* against the South.

emancipation   Freedom. The slaves were given their *emancipation*.

proclamation   An important statement. Abraham Lincoln signed the *Emancipation Proclamation* to free the slaves.

SLAVERY DIVIDES THE COUNTRY

In 1793 Eli Whitney invented a machine to help clean cotton. This machine was the cotton gin. It made cotton much easier to prepare for market. Planters could clean more cotton because of the cotton gin. Plantations became much bigger.

Southern plantations used many black slaves. They were used to working in tobacco and cotton fields. The planters wanted slavery to stay. They could not grow their crops cheaply without them. Even southerners who were poor believed in slavery. Slavery was part of their society. Plantation owners thought that they were protecting the slaves.

Slavery is not fair to the black people. Blacks did not want to be slaves. They were forced to be slaves. People from other parts of the country were against slavery. Many northerners wanted slavery stopped at once. They were called "abolitionists."

Many southerners were angry. They wanted the abolitionists to mind their own business. Planters said that they took good care of their slaves. They refused to see that slavery was bad.

But many northerners helped the slaves escape to freedom. They set up an "Underground Railway." "Underground" means "secret." The Underground Railway was not really a train. It was like stations on a real railway. It was a group of safe places for runaway slaves to hide. Thousands of slaves escaped by the Underground Railway.

FILL IN THE RIGHT ANSWER

Write *N* after each thing the North liked.
Write *S* after each thing the South liked.

Example: The invention of the cotton gin _____S_____

1. the Underground Railway _____
2. abolitionists _____
3. slavery _____
4. high tariffs _____

A WRITING ASSIGNMENT

Pretend that you are a slave. Write about your daily life. Remember — no electricity, TV, stereo, radio, or computers! They were not invented yet. Imagine that you worked on a plantation. Maybe you worked in the field picking cotton. Or maybe you worked in your master's big house washing dishes or sweeping floors. What was it like to be a slave?

WHICH WORD FITS?

Choose the correct answer.

The three main _____ (*parks, parts*) of the United States were the North, South, and West. They did not agree on many things.

A tariff is a _____ (*tax, sale*) on foreign goods. It makes the price of foreign goods higher. The North wanted a high tariff to protect its _____ (*factories, farms*). The South did not want a high tariff. It made prices _____ (*lower, higher*).

The West wanted _____ (*expensive, cheap*) roads and land. The North did not want to lose its workers. Factory owners were afraid. They thought that _____ (*workers, farmers*) would go west for free or cheap land.

The South wanted slavery. The invention of the cotton gin made cotton _____ (*harder, easier*) to grow. Plantations got very large. The slaves picked _____ (*cereal, cotton*) on the large plantations. Many people in the _____ (*North, South*) hated slavery. They wanted to stop it.

The United States was one _____ (*town, country*). But it had problems. The parts of the country did not agree. It was like an argument in a family.

Southerners talked about splitting away from the United States. They wanted to make a new country. The southern people even talked about war. This was like a divorce in a family.

Northerners were angry. They said that the Constitution does not let states leave the country. Northerners said that the United States is more important than the separate states. People from North and _____ (*South, East*) now talked about war.

WRITE A LETTER

Here are two letters. The first letter is from a southern plantation owner to a northern factory owner. The second letter is the northerner's answer. Finish both letters. Fill in the blanks with the right word.

Mr. Tom Drake
New York, NY

Dear Tom,

We have been _____ (fiends, friends) for almost twenty years. We are both _____ (cities, citizens) of the United States.

The people of the South are tired of northerners talking about _____ (slavery, salvation). We take good care of our _____ (sales, slaves). We must have slavery to run our large _____ (plants, plantations). Northerners are jealous. The North does not _____ (trust, treat) its workers fairly. Northern _____ (writers, workers) are paid very little. They have to work _____ (long, last) hours. Their _____ (rent, work) is often dangerous. Even young _____ (chickens, children) have to work.

Each _____ (state, slate) should decide whether it has slavery. The South will _____ (love, leave) the United States if we are forced to free our _____ (slaves, planters).

A war between North and South would be terrible. You are my best friend. _____ (Famines, Families) would be divided. I hope that this war never _____ (happens, helps).

Your old friend,
Jim Jackson

Northern Iron Works
New York, New York
November 30, 1860

Mr. Jim Jackson
Southern Stream Plantation
Cool River, Georgia

Dear Jim,

Thank you for your letter. I also _____ (hop, hope) that we do not have a war. I do not _____ (agree, ask) with you about northern workers. Our _____ (wonders, workers) can quit when they want. Your slaves are treated like _____ (property, poetry). Our workers are also not _____ (faced, forced) to work. They can go _____ (Waste, West) to get their own land. Our workers can even start their own _____ (buses, businesses).

I know many southerners. I _____ (know, no) that they are kind people. I cannot understand their _____ (feelings, fields) about slavery.

The United States is one _____ (country, county). _____ (States, Starts) do not have the right to leave it.

Your pal,
Tom Drake

THE FIGHTING STARTS

Abraham Lincoln was elected president in November, 1860. Many southerners were angry with Lincoln. They knew that Lincoln did not like slavery. Some southern states wanted to leave the Union. Lincoln wanted peace.

But the country was split. Leaders from the North and South were angry. They did not trust each other.

Seven southern states left the Union. These states were Alabama, Florida, Georgia, Louisiana, Mississippi, South Carolina, and Texas. They started a new country. They called it the "Confederate States of America."

Both sides built up their armies. The South attacked first. They asked a United States fort to surrender. This was Fort Sumter in South Carolina. The fort did not surrender. On April 12, 1861 the South attacked the fort. The North (United States) lost the fort. The Civil War was on!

TRUE OR FALSE?

Read the story.
Write *T* if the statement is true.
Write *F* if the statement is false.
Example: Abraham Lincoln was a president of the United States. _____T_____

1. Most southerners liked Abraham Lincoln. _____
2. The South fired the first shot of the Civil War. _____
3. The North saved Fort Sumter from the South. _____
4. Texas was one of the states that left the Union. _____
5. The Civil War was the war between the North and South. _____

Abraham Lincoln

A BLOODY WAR

Now one part of the United States was fighting another part. The two sides were not equal in strength. The North had more advantages. The North had more men, factories, and railroads. The North also had more ships. But the South fought on its own land. They had better generals.

The war lasted a long time. It was very bloody. The war divided families. Brothers fought brothers.

The North formed a blockade against the South. The blockade helped defeat the South. Ships covered with iron were used for the first time. The South built a ship called the *Merrimac*. It had iron plates. It was able to pass through the blockade. The *Merrimac* sunk many Union ships. The North built an iron ship called the *Monitor*. The two ships met and fought. After many hours, the *Merrimac* had to run back to port.

The North lost many battles at first. The South had a very great general. His name was Robert E. Lee. He won many victories against the North. President Lincoln had trouble getting a good general to lead the northern army. He finally found General Ulysses S. Grant.

General Grant was also a great general. He won many battles for the North. The North won two important battles on July 4, 1863. Vicksburg surrendered to Grant and the North won a great battle at Gettysburg, Pennsylvania.

President Lincoln gave a famous speech at Gettysburg. It was the Gettysburg Address. It is very short. But it is one of the most famous speeches in the world.

President Lincoln signed a paper to free the slaves during the war. It was called the "Emancipation Proclamation." It freed the slaves in states at war with the Union. There were no slaves in the Union.

The Civil War ended on April 9, 1865. General Lee met with General Grant to sign the surrender. They met at Appomatox Court House in Virginia. General Grant was kind to the South. He treated the southern army with kindness. Southern soldiers were allowed to keep their horses. General Grant did not let the Union soldiers fire a victory salute.

The long war proved that states cannot leave the Union when they want. The United States is one country. Each state is a permanent member of the country.

The War lasted four years. The South was in bad shape after the war. Confederate money had no value. Food, medicine, and clothing were scarce. Most of the fighting had been on southern soil. That is why so much of the South was ruined. The United States needed time to heal its wounds. There were many problems ahead.

WHICH WORD FITS?

Choose the right word.

1. The North had more _____ than the South.

    a. advantages   c. cotton
    b. tobacco   d. plantations

2. Ships covered with _____ were used for the first time in the Civil war.

    a. wood   c. iron
    b. plastic   d. wax

3. The North wanted to stop the South from getting supplies and selling cotton to other countries. The North formed a _____ against the South.

    a. proclamation   c. petition
    b. statement   d. blockade

4. At first, the South had better _____ than the North.

    a. factories   c. railroads
    b. clothing   d. generals

5. The South's main general was _____.

    a. Sherman   c. Lee
    b. Grant   d. Johnson

Bad Times

The South is having trouble. Food is in short supply. It is hard to get clothing. The northerners have stopped our shipments of food and clothing.

Most of the factories are in the North. They also have more railroads and soldiers. Our brave soldiers are fighting for our way of life. But they are losing many battles. Thousands of southern men have died and many more are wounded. We do not have enough doctors. We are short of medicine.

We must be as brave as our soldiers. We should not complain about shortages. Many of our fine southern women are helping out in hospitals. They are tending the wounded.

This is the time for all good people to come to the aid of our noble cause.

FILL IN THE RIGHT ANSWER

Answer these questions after reading the newspaper.

1. Is the message in this newspaper fact or opinion?_____
    Explain your answer._____
    _____

2. Does the writing show that the South is winning the Civil War?_____
    Explain your answer_____
    _____

3. What did the southern doctors not have that they needed ?_____
4. How are women helping to fight the war?_____
    _____

5. Why was it hard for the South to get food and clothing?

    _____

    _____

TRUE OR FALSE?

Read the story.
Write *T* if the statement is true.
Write *F* if the statement is false.

Example: The South won the Civil War. _____F_____

1. The North and South were about equal in strength. _____
2. Most of the battles were fought in the South. _____
3. The North's blockade stopped southern shipping of materials.
   _____
4. Robert E. Lee was a famous northern general. _____
5. It was easy for President Lincoln to find a good general. _____
6. The Gettysburg Address was President Lincoln's summer home.
   _____
7. The Emancipation Proclamation freed the slaves. _____
8. President Lincoln signed the Emancipation Proclamation during the Civil
   War. _____
9. The North won the Civil War. _____
10. The South was fighting to leave the Union. They wanted to start their own
    country. _____

FILL IN THE RIGHT ANSWER

Arrange these events in the right order. Write "1" after the first, "2" after the second, and so forth.

A. Fort Sumter is fired on by southern soldiers. _____
B. Abraham Lincoln gives his Gettysburg Address. _____
C. Eli Whitney invents the cotton gin. _____
D. Abraham Lincoln is elected President. _____
E. General Lee surrenders to General Grant. _____

LEARNING THE LANGUAGE

WHO, WHAT, WHEN, OR WHERE.

Phrases are parts of sentences. Look at the phrases that are underlined. Tell whether the underlined part of the sentence tells, **who, what, when,** or **where.** The first one is done for you.

1. Abraham Lincoln was president of the United States during the Civil War. _____when_____
2. A big battle was fought at Gettysburg, Pennsylvania. _____
3. We fought a war with England in 1812. _____
4. The Civil War was a long and bloody war. _____
5. Robert E. Lee was an important southern general. _____
6. The North had more factories than the South. _____
7. Most of the battles were fought in the South. _____
8. The Emancipation Proclamation freed the slaves. _____
9. General Lee surrendered to General Grant at Appomatox Court House in Virginia. _____
10. General Grant was kind to General Lee's army. _____